THE PRO

How To Become A Successful Footballer

Rory Winters

First published in the United Kingdom in 2023.

To my Family, Friends and Wife. Thank You for all of your continued belief and support.

To my Mentors, Coaches, Teammates and Opponents. Thank You for all of your lessons.

To Football. Thank You for enabling me to see the world.

CONTENTS

FOREWORD

by Thomas Beattie

From as far back as I can remember, football has always been a part of my DNA. Coming from a small, industrial town in Yorkshire, it was a positive outlet to express myself and it kept me away from some of the social pitfalls that many of my childhood friends succumbed to. At an early age, football became my saviour, or so I thought. I loved every part of the process of self-betterment, learning new skills and techniques that I would try and incorporate in to the game. The ball became my best friend, one that I took everywhere with me! I literally slept with a ball in my bed most nights growing up!As I progressed through the academy at Hull City, having being signed at 10 years old, I quickly started to learn how the sport I loved was actually a financially driven business. I was a tiny cog in a wheel that was ruthlessly focused on results. Nonetheless, the challenge excited me, whilst knowing I was constantly being assessed became a big part of my identity throughout life. This was fine in football but it wasn't as easy outside of the sport.Living in a small town had its benefits but one of the drawbacks was that everyone knew everyone else's business. It was especially glaring for the ones who were pursuing their dreams. Every time I stepped out of the house I felt I was being judged and analysed by everyone around me. I'd go to the supermarket with my mum, to be told I should have passed the ball more at the game over the weekend by the checkout lady! As a young lad, that frustrated the life out of me but it became something I used as a catalyst internally to prove people wrong. As I got older and continued to progress, the academy system at Hull signed some of the areas brightest talents, an environment I thrived in, and it gave me an added hunger to prove myself to my peers and coaches.When I turned 15, I was in my last year of high school and was selected to play in the reserves. Peter Taylor, who was also the England under 20 manager at the time, was the first team coach and he would often come to the reserve games to watch some of the younger lads. It was around this time that I started to struggle with my own personal identity, amplified by constantly being in a highly pressured environment. I remember playing against Sheffield United and feeling like I was in a hot bowl of soup. The confusion around my identity and orientation was making me feel like I was constantly running in to the wind, like I had lead in my boots.I'd been at the club for almost 10 years and it was every boys dream to live the life I was living and it was mine also, but something just felt off for me. Looking back now, at this point I just needed someone to put their arm around me and tell me what I was experiencing, that everything was going to be ok and that my uniqueness was my super power, not something to be afraid of. I longed for someone to see me as the person I was growing in to, instead of just the athlete or the asset. In the environment I was in, that felt miles away, and the disconnect I had with my own identity eventually became too much.The club

was great with me to be fair, but at the time I don't think they were equipped with the knowledge and awareness to understand, or even comprehend, what I was going through. Something that many clubs still don't have now!So I told my agent I wanted to leave the club. The management and I sat down and I told them I wanted to leave at the end of the season. I had no idea what would come next, I had fallen out of love with the one thing that always made me feel free and safe. Thankfully, my grades at school were very good and so I had an offer to attend university in America on a scholarship to study and play collegiately. I jumped at it! 4 weeks later I was in South Carolina! I couldn't even tell you where it was on the map of America.3 years later, I had become the programs most decorated student athlete in the history of the University, being named in the top 11 collegiate players in the country. Offers started to come flooding in for me to go back in to the professional game and continue the journey I set out on as a small boy from Yorkshire. This was the first time I had experienced life outside of the bubble I had been brought up in. I was starting to understand my own identity on and off the field, and this brought a heady mix of emotions. Going back in to the ruthless world of professional football knowing I was born in to a community that was misunderstood, discriminated against and looked at as a weakness petrified me.
Ultimately, after travelling the world playing in counties like Australia, Scotland, Norway, Albania and Canada, I arrived in Singapore, South East Asia. I had re-found the love of football again and was physically ready to take on the challenge. Although mentally I was still battling with my own personal identity, I buried it and poured every

ounce of energy I had in to football. My first true love, my source of comfort in a world of chaos, had been rekindled.I was blessed with the opportunity to see the world, using a round piece of leather, that has taken me to many areas of the globe. I met some amazing people along the way and it humbled me greatly and shaped me in to the person I am today.After winning the Singapore Premier League and qualifying for the Asians Champions League, we had the privilege of playing in many countries I had never dreamed of visiting. From Myanmar to Papua, Indonesia all the way to India and China. I remember walking out for the first champions league game in Myanmar and just thinking how on earth did I get here! As unorthodox as it was, I felt truly grateful for the opportunities football had provided me to be walking out on that pitch in a far flung corner of the world. Many emotions came flooding through my body after we played in Guangzhou, China. I felt a sense of loneliness and emptiness after the euphoria or playing in front of 40,000 people to sitting in my room alone. It was the first time I allowed myself to whisper to myself that I might be gay. It opened a whole box of questions that I didn't know how to answer, and didn't know who to turn to for advice. Who was I? What did I really want to do after this journey was owner? Is football all that I am?Shortly after, during a game back in Singapore, I sustained a head injury in a collision that abruptly forced me to finish the game that had provided for me, protected me, and been a huge piece of my identity for as long as I could remember!With multiple facial and skull fractures and a brain haemorrhage, I had to undergo many surgeries to regain a level of health that I was comfortable with. I call this my beautiful nightmare. I lost the first thing I ever loved, but I found myself in the process. I wasn't going to wake up another day and live a life to appease a group of people, I may, or may not, ever meet.During this process of figuring out who is Thomas Beattie, I embarked on a journey of entrepreneurship and business ownership. Jumping in to a new world with both feet, I began creating, building solutions, solving problems, using the tools I had acquired as a footballer.I had a new found love of building teams and bringing people together to compete in a new arena, the world of business. I felt free and had a blank canvas to create whatever I dreamed of. I began taking courses in entrepreneurship at places like Harvard and meeting inspiring business owners and mentors in a diverse range of industries. I felt like a child with the ball at my feet again! I still do.Fast forward another 4 years and I made the decision to speak about my identity publicly, to affect change in the sport that has given me so much and to be a catalyst for other players suffering in silence. It was one of the best decisions I have ever made. Controlling the narrative and setting myself free allowed me to use my voice and platform to really affect change and bring an added sense of purpose, to myself and to many others. The thing that once scared me the most suddenly became my super power. I quickly learned that our uniqueness is what makes us special. Not the amount of games I played for any given club or the accomplishments I achieved in football. As a child, most people just want to fit in, but at this point I realised being different is what makes us special.Football is a great teacher. It reveals and builds character, traits that carry over in to the world of business ownership. Perseverance, dedication, sacrifice and team work are all competencies that are required to achieve success, however you may define it, in any walk of life. Today, I'm still involved in the game but from a different perspective. Currently I'm looking at venturing in to ownership, as I've been able to build various companies that have allowed me the privilege to do so. It fills me with so much pride, knowing the journey to get here was anything but smooth sailing.I've been very fortunate to cross paths with many unbelievable individuals during my time in football, and Rory is definitely one of those. I've been able to witness first hand how he communicates, nurtures and challenges the players around him with so much conviction, but compassion also. I don't look back with regrets, but I often think if I had a mentor in the same mould as Rory, at various stages of my career, and life, I think I would have been able to learn to embrace my identity and not run from it, allowing me to fulfil my potential.One thing that Rory completely understands, and which took me a long time to realise, is that the mind is the professional. The body just follows what the mind tells it to do. Hence, being fully aware that being sharp, in control, and in a good mental state directly correlates with how we perform physically. Something I look back on now which strongly resonates with me is how being so confused and consumed by a failure to understand my own identity had such a profound effect on me physically, on and off the field.Football is one of those funny careers. It can bring you the highest of highs and the lowest of lows. It can take you to all corners of the world and it can allow you to cross paths with people who will become lifelong friends. It will push you to your limits. It will be a teacher of many things and it will, at times, break you. But, underneath it all, it's still just a game. A game that taught me many life lessons, and for this, I will be eternally grateful.

I hope you can take the wisdom and guidance offered by Rory in this book and implement some of the lessons in your own footballing journey. Success is defined by you and you alone, not what society expects or other people demand of you. As you'll read, Rory has lived a life full of adventure and the inevitable ups and downs any footballer faces. I highly encourage you to learn from his story and the lessons he shares in the pages ahead.

Thomas

PROLOGUE

"Pro, Hey, Pro…Is that you? What are you doing here?"

The Pro's heart sank, his stomach dropping as though on a rollercoaster. He ignored the friendly acknowledgement fired at him from the dense queue at the other side of the counter. Tucking his chin to his chest, pulling the cap lower and tighter to shade his features.

"Oh, are you doing this for the football in the community programme, Pro?"

It hit him hard, like blocking a fierce shot on a cold winter's day. He sucked in a deep breath, composing himself, all the while hoping that the floor beneath his once lauded feet would swallow him whole. Looking up, feeling worse than if he'd just scored an own goal in a cup final, his heavy eyes met the voice that had called to him.

"Rob, how are you mate? Nah, this is me for now mate…" he trailed off, looking down in shame once again.

"Jeez Pro, well, let me know if you want a job down at the supermarket, I know the fruit and veg counter need some extra hands..."

"Yeah, maybe mate, thanks..."

The Pro tensed up, felt every sinew in his body squeeze tight, as the incessant buzz of the unfamiliar fluorescent lights beat down on his brow. Only two weeks ago it had been a busy stadium under the floodlights. Now, this.

"Can I get a Big Mac meal, Coke please...yeah, Thanks" his old school friend places his order as, at the same time, The Pro turns back to the shelves of McNuggets, Fillet of Fish and gives the trays a shake. He sighs again, trying to dissipate the tension and shame consuming him.

"See you around Pro, and get in touch yeah?" Rob shouted, swinging his Big Mac meal in his left hand as begins to schlurp at the Coke in his right hand, half waving.

"Yeah, will do, see you Rob" muttered The Pro, barely audible. He knew at this point that his secret was out. In the small city he was raised and was now back in, word spread quick, especially if it was negative. His remaining strength, limited as it was, drains further still.

An accusatory tap on his shoulder from behind jolts him from his ennui.

"You...Hello, anyone in there? Make yourself useful and go and clean the gherkin and sauces out in the back room, I'll take over here, customers are waiting…" hissed the manager, an angry man with a greasy complexion and bitter features, "You just can't get the staff anywhere these days…"

The Pro resigns himself to the task at hand, too weak to argue and too frayed to fight back with indignance. The overpowering scent of grease and gherkins combine with this glum reality to make a soup of sadness. He grabs the jet wash tap and begins to blitz the dirty pots, the gherkin juice spraying like champagne, splashing at his standard issue McDonalds apron.

CHAPTER 1: ENJOY THE GAME

As soon as he stumbled up to his feet and took his first steps, Rory Winters was kicking a ball. In fact, he was more comfortable kicking than crawling in his first year, and by his second year on earth it was his powerful kicking that awed people, rather than the usual development markers of walking and talking, both of which came at the usual rate of the average infant.

That their first-born son showed an adept athleticismcame as a surprise to his parents, both young and more artistic than sporting. Raised in a small, post-industrial town in the North of England, where the rain seemed to consistently coat the tightly packed houses in a dark and wet glaze, Rory couldn't be kept inside for long. Each day consisted of him sneaking through the cramped, claustrophobic concrete yard at the back of the small terraced house to the shattered glass strewn alleyway beyond, ball under his arm and football kit getting drenched in the downpour.

His adept escapology may have been a trait inherited from his Dad, a moonlighting magician, who spent long spells of Rory's formative years on far-flung working assignments to faraway parts of the country. This left just him and his Mum together a lot of the time, her doing her best to manage the both of them whilst juggling life as a trainee teacher, Rory finding more solace in kicking a football than anything else. When his Dad did return, he and Rory kicked a ball together, his Dad surprised by the power his small son possessed in his tiny feet, the accuracy of his aim, all the while oblivious to the actual aptitude his son had. Rory cherished these moments of bonding with his Dad, showcasing his skills learnt in isolation, just him, the wall, the alleyway where he'd won the World Cup all on his own a thousand times, scored the winning goal in the FA Cup Final in his fantastical world. When his Dad left for work again after a day or two, he would kick the ball with more ferociousness against the bricks until exhaustion, then sit down with his back against the wall, tears streaming down his cheeks, feeling like the whole world was against him.

Lesson 1: ENJOY THE GAME

Football is a game, a love of which is often developed in childhood through its beautiful simplicity. I could kick a pair of socks in the house, a stone on the pavement, a 'flyaway' ball on the park, an empty soft drink can in the alleyway. A ball wasn't always necessary, and honing my skills on the 'street' enables me to have thousands of touches of pretty much any moveable object. As I grew older, that almost inherent desire to kick things transferred into being a reasonably talented footballer. But it was always the fun and enjoyment of kicking something with the carefree fantastical world that children occupy that compelled me to love the game. I won more World Cups in that back alleyway for England, more Premier Leagues, FA Cups and Champions League than would be possible

in the next century of real time life. I was the players, the fans, the commentators. I enjoyed it. It was exciting. I loved it!
Never forget why you started to love football. Keep the childlike enjoyment and fun when things start to get serious. It's impossible to beat someone who has fun at what they do.

CHAPTER 2: CREATE YOUR MANTRA

By the age of 6, Rory's Dad was working locally on a permanent basis, whilst his Mum had given birth to a little girl, a new sister. Rory was developing his kicking ability at an exponential rate. The alleyway, with its cobblestones filled with broken beer bottles and brick walls adorned in gang graffiti, had become too small for his skills. His Dad had drawn rings on the wall in white paint, target practice. The red brick inside each circle was beginning to crumble from the consistent pounding it took from the football. For his 7th birthday, his Grandad bought him his first pair of real football boots, a pair of black Arrow's with moulded rubber studs and long laces that had to be double knotted. Rory didn't take them off his feet, or the smile off his face, for a week, even sleeping in them. He felt like the coolest kid in town.

Things got even more incredible soon after. His Grandad, who had encouraged him to develop his footballing ability indoors with a small sponge ball, much to the chagrin of his Grandma, took him to Old Trafford to watch

Manchester United play in the Premier League. Sandwiched between his Grandads legs, he sneaked through the turnstiles smoothly and spent the next 3 hours engrossed by the sights, sounds and smells of a huge stadium and the spectacle of the game. If he hadn't already been in love with football, he certainly was now. From that point on, Sunday mornings were spent watching Match of the Day reruns instead of cartoons, he sold all of his Batman toys at a car boot sale and spent the cash he'd made on a new England football shirt and also collected football stickers with a fervent passion, completing countless chores around the house so he could earn some small change for another pack. He was obsessed. It was time for Rory to enter the real world, to be pitted against other boys and girls who loved football and practiced kicking too.

On Saturday mornings he and his Dad went to the local leisure centre, to a structured football session for children his age. After 3 weeks, Rory had proven that his ability far surpassed that of the other children, that his first session wasn't a lucky coincidence and that his awareness within the confines of the small pitch accelerated at lightning quick speed. During the school summer holiday of that year, he was taken by his Mum and Grandparents to a weeklong football camp in a nearby town, where the sun broke through the clouds and he continued to shine brighter than any other with a football at his feet. He was kicked, tripped and flipped by the other boys but bounced back up and carried on, his love for the game growing with each tackle he evaded, each pass he made and each goal he scored.

It was at this sun-drenched camp, where the heat danced off the grass in a hallucinatory haze, that Rory was asked by an impressed coach to join a team, his first actual team. A week later, a dark, brooding storm shattered the sun kissed summer, rolling black clouds dumping a deluge of heavy rain onto the old, spluttering car Rory and his Dad drove to his first game. As the deafening downpour increased in intensity, bouncing off the cars roof, his Dad pulled to a stop near the pitch, the other boys running gleefully in the rain, getting ready to kick off.

"I can't, I don't want to play…" Rory announced, inaudible under the din of the torrential rain.

His Dad opened the door, ruffling Rory's hair. Rory sank into his seat.

"C'mon mate, it's only a bit of rain"

Rory stayed frozen to the chair, small and still.

"I don't want to; I feel really sick…"

"It's alright mate, that's just nerves, c'mon"

Rooted to the chair, Rory didn't move. The rain continued. His Dads black hair dripped cold rain onto his chair as he bent over and into the driver's seat.

"Listen, we can go back home and that's ok. But we're here so you might as well give it a go? What d'you think?" motioned his Dad as an electric surge of lightning crackled overhead, illuminating the pitch and the ball through the gloom.

12 months later, Rory is on a stage. He holds the Players and Mangers Player of the Year trophies in his hands after a season in which he continues to excel as a young

footballer amongst his peers. He doesn't know where to look, his shy demeanour visibly shrinking at the applause, by the attention, the reluctant star of the team, who lets his feet do most of his talking.

The same sodden city. The same spluttering car. The sister fidgeting with her doll in her hands, looking out of the steaming window as the car's engine struggled to start after stopping at a traffic light. A new addition, a baby brother, wrestled uncomfortably in a car seat. In his Mum's hands a letter, stamped with the team badge of the local professional football club. Rory had attended a summer trial with the club, a week of intensive training with a chance to sign if you were talented enough for the season ahead. From the passenger seat, his Mum slides her finger under the seal. For Rory, time has stopped. There is palpable tension inside the car, anticipation, an anxious energy. Rory is only 8 years old.

"Rory done well. We would like to sign him for the upcoming season and develop him further as a footballer at our academy."

The rain stops. The car starts. The steam clears. The doll in his sister's hands dances in her glee, his baby brother calms, his family drive in a united joy. Everything seems fixed, the brightness shines through the clouds. It's a good day.

The attached player report details Rory's superpowers as mainly A's, shooting, passing, strength. All told, he is regarded as an A in 15 of the 29 measurable metrics the coach has to assess the young man with. As the car pulls to a halt on the narrow street, as the drizzle begins again, he is already racing out of the yard and into the familiar old alleyway. The fading white circles on the wall, the crumbling bricks, the smashed glass between the cobbles, it's all beautiful, it's all played a part in this day, a day in which his whole family was brought together in a blissful joy by his footballing abilities, where smiles and laughs were shared and his hours upon hours of isolated practice led to his selection.

Lesson 2: Create Your Mantra

The trials and tribulations of a footballer start early. The nerves, and the management of such nerves, often afflict many footballers at all stages of their career and all levels of the game. I was a nervous wreck before that first game as a 7-year-old. I was a nervous ball of energy on trial at my hometown club. By the time I signed my first contract, at the crazily young age of 8, I had a mantra with my Dad before each game which kept my nerves in check and framed them positively. This was the mantra, shouted in the car before every game...

Dad, "What do we want?"
Me, "To play my best?"
Dad, "When do we want it?"
Me, "Now!"
Dad, "What do we want?"
Me, "To score a goal!"
Dad, "When do we want it?"
Me, "Now!"
Both, "Yeeeeeeeeaaaaahhhhhh!"

As a young boy all I could do is play to the best of my ability that day. It was important that I didn't ever feel any pressure from my Dad to be the best player on the pitch, he only asked I tried my best. For that I'm fortunate. As for the goal, as a defender that was a difficult one, but sometimes it did happen. This mantra was one way of regulating my nervous system, analysing the task ahead and setting a reasonable target for the game, thus relieving the sickening nerves and allowing them to be an ingredient to help rather than hinder my performance.

Coming up with your own mantra is something I encourage you to do. You see it at the elite level of most sports, from Rafa Nadal's pre point twitch in tennis to Owen Farrell's laser like focus in Rugby to Cristiano Ronaldo's stance before a free kick. These personal mantras and performance routines regulate the nervous system and enable clarity on the task at hand. Whether it's during a game like these guys or before a game like me, the benefit of assuming control of your nerves can only help improve your performance in any given task.

CHAPTER 3: A HEALTHY CHALLENGE

It soon became clear that Rory wasn't the only kid with consistently good kicking in their small city. At the academy, there was a team of twenty young boys, all with terrific talent with a ball at their feet. It was here, over the span of the next 7 years, from young boy to young man, that Rory learnt quickly how to develop and use his powers, how to compete, how to win, how to lose and how to defend. Games each Sunday against other academies, mile after mile in the car and hours honing his craft. Top tier tournaments tested his mettle. Teammates came and went, signed and released, trialled and thrown out.

The team has a succession of coaches, recently retired senior professionals desperately seeking a sustainable way to stay in the sport, who saw potential in him. They admired his composure on the ball, his reading of the game, his strength and aggression, whilst cutting him down to size with criticism of his communication. An obvious weakness in his arsenal, the young boy struggled to grasp the importance of speaking on the pitch, much to the frustration of coach after coach.

As he entered adolescence and maturation began, he grew taller and less coordinated until eventually it settled and he found that he was faster and stronger than ever before. A huge surge of power had been delivered to his legs. allowing him to strike a ball further and to jump higher to win more headers. At 14, he was excelling amongst his peers and was moved up an age group to play with older boys. The same powers he exuded in his own age group were monstrously mitigated, bigger boys and stolen superpowers. He was normal again, his passing average, his composure crumbling under the pressure, his deafening silence screaming as the games went by in a blur. He spent much of the rest of the season sat on the side-lines, playing 20 minutes here and there, stalling his progress. The deep dive to accelerated development had drowned him, disintegrated his superpowers, doused him in despair. Spluttering like the family car, he just about made it through the rest of the season, hoping against hope to be back with his own age group, comfortable confines. The young boy, turning into a young man, was only human after all.

Lesson 3: A Healthy Challenge

To be selected to become a Royal Marine and wear the coveted Green Beret is one of the toughest challenges in the Military world. Similar challenges exist in the US Navy Seals and the Nepalese Ghurkhas. The rigorous, hellish and relentless selection process is designed to weed out those who would let down the team in battle. None of these armed forces can afford to carry a weak member of the team when behind enemy lines or undertaking a mission to recover hostages for example. In the Royal Marines the candidates are put under immense pressure from minute one of the selection process, with the 32-week training regime including some of the hardest physical and mental tasks the human mind and body can tolerate. Those who progress through each challenge and eventually receive the green beret are then classed as an elite band of commando's, prepared to undertake some of the most brutal of military appointments. Those who drop out are not deemed failures, although they don't have the abilities needed to reach this elite level.

Although academy football is a much tamer beast than the Royal Marines Commando training, there are similarities in the process to gaining elite status in both disciplines. Young players will be thrust into high pressure situations from the age of 8, will have to compete with and against the other best young players in the country, be constantly assessed and challenged. Ultimately, they will either successfully progress to the next stage of their development at the end of each season, or be let go and cut adrift from the system they have dedicated so much energy, time and effort to. There are a few notable fears the Marine Commando will face throughout their training process. One is dropping out as they can't handle the incessant demands of being a recruit, another is to be back-trooped if they fail a certain stage and have to sit that stage again. A footballer experiences similar fears on their way to the top.

Atevery academy, every time a player walks into the building, they are being assessed, from their demeanour to their coachability to their performances in physical testing. They will be asked to play different positions and, in some cases, like I was, asked to step up a level to see how they cope. The real threat of injury is ever present for any athlete and a pertinent issue in football is the physical maturation of young players through their adolescent years. To remain mentally strong, resilient through adversity and to cope with the pressure academy football can present to young people is a sure- fire way of growing up quickly. All those in the academy system enter a dog-eat-dog culture which is very unforgiving and ruthless in its processes. Each training session, game or even whole season is an opportunity to learn and grow, whatever the final outcome may be. Talent obviously gets a young footballer through the door of an academy, yet the ability to be coachable and to willingly learn is often the difference between those who sustain relative success on the journey and those who fall by the wayside. It's imperative that a heady dose of humbleness and work ethic supplement the young footballers talent in order for them to successfully implement the many lessons football will teach them in a positive manner for the rest of their lives.

CHAPTER 4: BE READY

Fast forward a year. By the age of 15, when decisions on professional contracts approach on the horizon, Rory had regained his confidence, and with it his superpowers. Away from the club he is captain of his school team, his town team and starring for his county team too.

The day everything changed forever, the young man was at a school summer fair with his friends, a blistering hot day in early July. The scent of burgers and hot dogs sizzling in the sun, the lads spend an hour bobbing unsuccessfully round the traditional fair games, the Tombola, the coconut shine, hook a duck, leaving each stall empty handed until they stumbled upon the penalty shoot-out game.

"Go on, win us something Roars" Andy encourages him
"Yeah, go on..." reaffirms Dave,
"He's rubbish anyway, he won't get it..." sniggers Adam, the wind-up merchant of the group.

Rory's eyes flash with anger at Adam's comment, his best mates knowing that exactly that comment, of not being good enough, is what will convince him to take the shot and win them something, anything.

"Go on then..." as he hands over his last pound coin to the stall owner, picking up the half flat ball and placing it on the scuffed spot.

"OK son, you've three go's. Hit the cut out in the top corner you get that box of sweets, hit two of the bottom corners you get the goldfish, hit the big hole in the middle, well, you can have some candyfloss. All 3, you get the star prize"

"What's that then?" asks Adam as his eyes light up, knowing that they could well be walking away with whatever it might be.

The shop owner pulls out a crumpled £20 note from his stained jeans, grinning wildly as he winks,

"Good luck son", putting the money back in his pocket with a smug grin and a knowing tap.

Bang! One out of one. Straight down the middle, he watches Dave grab a stick of candyfloss, the pink sugar sticking to his chin as he wolfs it down whilst the stall owner's crooked teeth smile inside his curling lips.

Boom! In goes the second, nestling in the bottom left corner. The stall owner sneers as he eyes up the string of sad goldfish floating in plastic bags, selecting the smallest and somersaulting it through the sky to Andy, who barely catches it in a flustered panic before staring lovingly at the fish swimming in circles in its tiny world of warm water.

“Make sure you look after it kid…delicate things they are them goldfish” chuckles the creepy stall owner, disappointed that he had seemingly picked the cricketer of the group to throw the fish to.

The footballer places the ball down on the spot again. The stall owner digs into his pocket once again, unfolding the dusty note and fluttering it above his head.

“No chance kid, no chance...” his statement belying his evident fear, his beady eyes blinking as a single bead of sweat trickled down his left temple, his pulse visible under his sinewy neck and his grasp on the note firm.

He takes a deep breath and stands tall, his laser focus, honed in the alleyway for years, directed from ball to top right corner, ball to top left corner. He takes four steps back, knowing he’s going to strike the ball into the top right corner, with his left foot, the same one that was assessed as weak 7 years ago in his first report. Another deep breath, he’s all flow as his friends stand frozen in time, spending the £20 already at the chippy down the road. As he looks up again at the top right corner, lifting his left foot to start his run up, a strong vibration reverberates in his pocket, ring tone piercing the suspense.

“Noooooooooo, leave it…” insists Adam.
“Take the shot kid...” says the delighted stall owner, clutching the cash close.
“Go on mate, get us the prize first ...” demands Dave.

He stops his run up and takes his phone from his pocket. Mum flashes on the screen. Typical.

He lifts the phone to his ear.

“Mum, I’m in the middle of something… yeah but ill ring you back in a minute. Oh, come on...what, who did? Really? Oh, ok, yeah...yeah...will do...Wow! Ok I’ll be back quick!”

He puts the phone down, jams it in his pocket and looks at the inquisitive faces of his friends.

“Sorry lads, I’ve got to go…” as he breaks into a stride, bolting off away from the fair, across the field as the stall owners sinister cackle rises in volume, his friends stood in disbelief as the money disappears into the vortex of the pocket after Adam takes the final shot and hits the ball way wide and way over the target, coming to a stop forty yards away underneath the merry go round ride.

“Now go and get me that ball you little...” shouts the stall holder at Adam, who skulks off, distraught at the miss.

Rory gets home in record timing. Breathlessly he slams at the front door,

“Are you being serious?”
“Yes, you’ve to meet at the stadium tomorrow at 1pm, the games at 3. Just need boots and shinpads, they have everything else for you...”

His stomach drops, on the rollercoaster again, but this time he’s enjoying the ride, his hands in the air.

24 hours later he makes his debut for the first team in their opening pre-season friendly against a local semi professional team. Rory is 15, with 1 week left in Year 10 at school before the summer holidays start. Only two months earlier he had been amongst the thousands of fans watching the very players he's now on the same team as playing in the Play-off final for a chance at promotion to the Premier League. Things happen fast in football it seems.

The compact changing room is filled with the athletic prowess of international footballers and new signings, the smell of liniment oil and sweat, matched by the bass of the sound system, sneaking under the door that's shut tight for the team talk. Beyond, the stadium is filling up with fans, eager to see their team start a new season. It's the real deal. New kit laid out ready, more water, energy drinks and jelly babies than the local supermarket, footballs freshly inflated and the latest boots being laced up. Rory plays 45 minutes, the second half, as the team canter to an easy win. His adrenaline gets him through the game, his fitness and strength shook playing against angry grown men with a point to prove. Despite not performing to his best, he struggles to sleep in the evenings muggy heat, sweating and smiling.

At school on Monday, he is greeted as a hero by his mates, loved by the majority, loathed by the jealous minority and no longer lesser known by those who couldn't care less about football. On the corridors between lessons, he hears the whisper emerge from the shadows,
"That's The Pro" as younger children gaze up at him, in awe. It spreads quick. The girls in his year mock him with

it, his mates adopt the nickname for him. That day 'The Pro' is born. When his sister gets home, she tells the family she is now known as 'The Pro's" sister, not by her actual name. The reluctant superhero, he flushes red with embarrassment each time he hears his new nickname, but he walks taller all the same for the remainder of the last week of the school year.

Lesson 4: Be Ready

In 2019 I had the opportunity to travel with a group of friends to Nepal, the aim being to trek for 21 days through the Annapurna mountain range, near the world-renowned Mount Everest. Every part of my adventurous spirit wanted to join them; in fact, it was a no brainer for me. I had been through a tough year on a personal level and could have done with the fresh mountain air, no phone signal and that blissful, vast landscape. The problem however was that I was not prepared. Physically, mentally or emotionally, I wasn't fit to trek for 7 days, never mind 21. My friends had trained under my tutelage for 6 months in the lead up to the trek, putting in the hours as I coached them how to conquer mountains with squats, deadlifts and an untold amount of stair climbs whilst I went through the motions with my own training.

I didn't go. Instead, I waved the group of intrepid explorers off at the airport and looked after their pet dogs for the three weeks. Shrouded with disappointment and with the famous competitive streak every footballer possesses biting at my consciousness, I was left with a sense of bitterness at not being on the journey with them rather than pride at seeing them ascend peak upon peak.

Finally, I learnt the lesson that I should have learnt aged 15 with the first team. I wasn't prepared.

In the off season when I was 15, I behaved the same as most other young people my age, rather than a young footballer. I ate rubbish food; I kicked a ball in the park and on the schoolyard but I didn't do any extra training. I played on the PlayStation until the early hours each weekend and discovered my attraction to the opposite sex and the associated peacocking that many teenagers exhibit in puberty. I was about to win £20 by kicking a ball at a funfair when my Mum called with the news of my selection and had no doubt been to the chippy that lunchtime for a bag of chips and curry sauce. I was being a kid, which was totally acceptable, but I had the ambition and real chance to be a professional footballer. I'd switched off and I really wasn't ready to be thrust into a game against grown men on a team with seasoned professionals who took care of themselves in the off season. It was my own fault and although I didn't let that happen again in football terms, the Annapurna trip was another reminder that it's critical, whether that's on the field or scaling a mountain, to be proactive than reactive in order to reach top.

CHAPTER 5: RIDE THE WAVES

In an induction talk at the start of that next season for parents and players, The Pro officially enters the pivotal under 16's. All the selected hopeful footballing stars of the future were made aware that they were representing a professional club, with the sole aim to produce professional footballers for the first team. Although The Pro, nor his parents, knew at the time, The Pro was selected as part of a ploy by the club to trawl the town for talent, fish in a plastic bag, lambs to slaughter.

It's soon November, a wicked wind blows into the city from the nearby North Sea coast, tearing down trees and leaving debris careering across the roads. That evening, after an extra GCSE revision class at school, The Pro has one of the thrice weekly scheduled training sessions at the academy. Competition is reaching boiling point within the squad, as torrents of trialists come in from the bigger clubs in the area, everyone fighting for a contract with all their might. Even the warm-ups have become battlegrounds. The Pro still possesses a rhythmic reading of the game, a reliable range of passes and a rigid defensive skillset.

Confident he is on track to secure a contract, The Pro keeps doing what he is best at, safe in the belief that he will be selected by the staff, destined for the bright lights of the first team on a regular basis, a future hometown hero.

As soon as his Dad returned home from work, he told The Pro about the call he received earlier that day from the newly appointed Head of the Academy, who had asked The Pro to attend training that evening not in the usual kit but instead in the matchday tracksuit, with no need to bring boots along as it's just a meeting for him. A smile breaks across both of their faces. This must be it, decision day, youth team contract to be offered, a huge leap closer to the first team. An acceleration of adrenaline shoots through his body, igniting his energy and sending shockwaves of confidence to every extremity.

Wearing the bright red club tracksuit, he straps on his seatbelt in the same old spluttering family car and they set off, diverted from the familiar route by the detritus and debris from the storm, avoiding the disarray that's dropped from the sky to the streets in howling wind.
Once again, the car creaks to a stop, a poignant signpost in The Pro's footballing journey. He and his Dad get out and slam the car doors behind them, anticipation and excitement building. The convictionof the inevitable impending offer of a contract forming a shielding halo around them from the vicious weather. They walk past the rest of his team who are training already, yet more new and unfamiliar trialists faces amongst the old guard of players he's played alongside for years. In their old teams training kit, the hopefuls look mismatched in their

desperation to impress the coach in the hour and a half they have. All bluster and noise. He breathes a sigh of relief, no longer fearing the competition. They reach the Head Coach's office door, the warm glow of the yellow lights beckoning them in from the harsh, darkening night outside.

Seated in the hard, plastic chairs, it takes only one minute, after the pleasantries, for The Pro to learn his fate.

"We don't believe that you have the ability to be a Premier League footballer..." is all The Pro hears, before he momentarily mentally departs the room.

"But you're not a Premier League club" his Dad counters, somewhat incredulous at seeing 7 years of his son's sacrifices swept away in a single statement.

The rain pounds the roof of the office, creating a din of sound rendering the rest of the Head Coach's tactile speech indecipherable. The ferocious wind wraps its dangerous profile around the portacabin, shaking the foundations. A pathetic fallacy. The room spins, seemingly lifted up and away from terra firma, swirling in the sky before smashing back to down earth with a devastating crash, bang, wallop. The Pro, for the briefest of moments, is back in the room. He blinks the tears back, holding together the pieces of his pride whilst the pen shakes in his unsteady grip, signing his release form. Promises emanate from the Head Coach's mouth, false liquid gold to the shattered hearts of the Dad and son sat across from him. The promises flow quickly, inspiring a belief in the chaos that this will be Ok, that the club still cares; Trials at other clubs, check in calls, aftercare programme, glowing references, a place to train 'til you find somewhere else. It is all The Pro has to cling on to as his dream career turns into the same driftwood that he sees laying destitute on the banks of the overflowing river as they drive home. His family consoles him, wrapping him up in their comforting cocoon of commiserating kinship. His tears roll, his heart can't be pieced back together by their love. Shame ripples through his core, exacerbated the following day at school after a sleepless night fraught with anger and confusion.

Not one of the promises made by the Head of the Academy is fulfilled.

Lesson 5: Ride the Waves

If you ever get a chance to have a go at surfing, I highly encourage you to get out into the waves and try it out. A couple of years ago I overcame my fear of water, due to my inability to swim very well, by getting on a surf board and trying to stay on it. It was a long two hours. I wanted to give up countless times, I was crushed under and smashed around by the powerful waves, the breath was taken out of me and I was covered in scrapes and bruises. I can say that I got up on the board and successfully rode a wave a grand total of twice in 2 hours. Finding the strength to grab back hold of the board, paddle out beyond the break, get back up on your feet before crashing back into the ferocious waves again and being spat out on the beach in what feels like an eternity, but is actually just 2 or 3 seconds, is truly both humbling and exhilarating at the same time.

It struck a chord with me as it instantly reminded me of the journey of a young footballer. The excitement of getting into the water; when you first get scouted, signing your first contract, the anticipation of a great career ahead as you progress further into the academy system. Next come the small waves you really learn to ride in, with inevitable falls and mistakes made; the trialist who plays in your position, being dropped to the bench, a loss of form, an unsettled home life, social pressure, an injury, all throw you off the board into the waves. It takes strength to get back out there, to try again after a bad experience. Then comes the real test. You keep progressing and you move to the bigger break, with bigger waves, the real deal. You get on the board, confident you can do it, buoyed by your previous mastery of the smaller waves. The big wave feels manageable at first, then it builds momentum and you're in a state of shock, bang! You are smashed into the unrelenting sea; You're dropped, you're released, you aren't good enough, you're rejected at trial after trial, you want to give up. And many people do. Why would you choose to go back out there into the danger zone?

It's at this point that you will find out if you still want to ride the wave. There is no shame in saying no and getting out of the water. There is no superiority to be claimed in going back out into the waves, as they won't stop coming. In a football career, you have to keep getting back on that board, knowing the waves will always come, some big, some small, but all there to challenge you and sometimes, carry you into something bigger than yourself. You've swallowed enough sea water and been battered around enough to no longer find it fun. I got out of the water having learnt tonnes, but not achieved all I had envisaged at the start of the surf lesson and I was at peace with that.

CHAPTER 6: CAN'T STOP, WON'T STOP

He's written, stamped and posted letters to every club in England and Scotland, pleading for a chance. Only one has the decency to reply. Unfortunately, they have already selected their squad, but will keep his name on file for the scouting team. With all of his might, a week after being released, The Pro was back on a pitch, mustering up what courage he has left to play for his county team in the National Cup Final. After the game, two scouts are lingering by his Dad's car, their dark silhouettes drawing long shadows across the dimly lit car park, their breath rising into the air, momentarily concealing the stars in the clear night sky above.

Upon their targets approach, the scouts scurry onto their feet, bracing their bodies as they turn into the cold and revealing the club crests emblazoned over their heart. One face is familiar to The Pro's Dad, having also recently scouted The Pro's younger brother for the same Premier League club he represents here in the car park. At just 6 years of age, his younger brother is already coveted by almost every football club in the North West of England. It seems the tentacles of this ruthless business extend further and further to trap their increasingly younger prey, beckoning them forward with a famously familiar badge, before releasing the lethal venom of crushed dreams on these impressionable youngsters and their parents in ruthless displays of disdain.

"See your brothers doing well son...and well played tonight, no idea why they let you go..." begins the Premier League scout.

"Aye, poor decision if I've ever seen one that is, well done son, I'm Mark, nice to meet you, and you, Sir" cut in the lower league team scout, offering his cold hand to The Pro and his Dad.

"So, listen, both of us here would like to take you in to our clubs, have a look at you for six weeks and see if you can get yourself a contract..." starts the Premier League scout again.

"Yep, that's right, but obviously you can't do both at the same time son" butts in the lower league scout before continuing,

"So, here's my pitch. No doubt about it, you'll get your contract offer within a week or two. But, and more importantly, we're winning everything in front of us, five lads made their debut already this season. We need you kids to keep the club afloat, sell you back to them idiots who let you go eh?"

"Well, I can't argue with that" grimaces the Premier League scout to The Pro's Dad.
"But I can say that I believe you've a big chance of getting signed, they all already know who you are. 6 weeks with us and if you don't get a deal then you can go there anyway" he gestures at Mark.

"Don't bank on it son, the contracts are being handed out already, times ticking on. Another 6 weeks of who knows what with the big boys with their fancy facilities and you might even get a bit too soft. So, what do you say? Come and get something secured with us, they'll buy you if they want you that much" coerces Mark.

"Hey, take a day or two to think about it kid, your Dad has my number and we can sort it out if you want to come in for 6 weeks..." suggests the Premier League scout, diffusing any tension with a knowing glance at the adults in the conversation before winking at The Pro and heading off to his car, tutting to himself at Mark's crass sales pitch.

"We train tomorrow night son, let's get your future sorted then you can get them exams done, not that you'll be needing them as a footballer eh, don't worry about them and focus on your football" urges Mark, parroting footballs familiar contempt for education alongside playing.

It's a one-hour drive in the crumbling car to the trial. The Pro is alone. The accents are different, the territory unfamiliar and his Sports Direct Sondico kit singles him out even further from the lads in their official club kit. He stands isolated, shivering at the side of the pitch, his silent demeanour underscored by the icy cold. He's quickly abecome a frozen juxtaposition. Nervous but apathetic, he doesn't want to be here, yet where else would he rather be? His Dad didn't need to convince him to get out of the car this time, but it took a deep breath and steely determination, rather than their usual pre match ritual of the 'What do we want?' mantra to walk up the steps to the dilapidated sports centre, the single light illuminating the path, flickering in its own indifference at finding itself in this place as the frost laid itself down on the surfaces of any solid object it found.

"Hey son, good to see you, great decision!" bellows Mark from the other side of the AstroTurf pitch. The Pro cringes.

"Come over son, meet Tommy, he'll love you...Tommy, this is Rory, he's a tough little bugger, not much will beat him, but could probably do with a kick up the backside to speed up, sometimes he's so relaxed on the ball he might fall asleep..." explains Mark to a short, serious looking Scotsman who introduces himself as Tommy, u16 Head Coach.

"Alright son, that's the lads over there, go an' introduce y'self tae em" instructs Tommy, gesturing at the group of lads playing keep ball in the corner of the pitch, raucous and loud as they wait for the younger age groups to finish their session and vacate that area of the pitch.

Two weeks later, as Mark had predicted, The Pro is offered a 2-year professional apprenticeship with the lower league club. This renders any opportunity to trial and 'become soft' at the Premier League club impossible, until he was "sold there, anyway", Mark added whilst watching him sign the forms, eyes glinting with the discovery fee he was about to cash in. The Pro had made things look easy, impressing his new coach Tommy and his teammates quickly, settling into the surroundings like the old back alleyway.

He had done it. He had taken one step back to jump two forwards. His talents had been selected. He was The Pro again, his pride somewhat restored. The rejection no longer raged in flames, but smouldered, doused by the sheer resilience of picking himself up and fighting again to reclaim his powers from the scrapyard they'd been discarded on by his release. At school, so called friends, who had enjoyed his fall from grace a little too much after his release, became interested in him again. With the kick in confidence, his superpowers, which seemed to have waned - he even looked average playing football on the yard at breaktime- slowly returned. He had a stride back in his step.

Lesson 6: Can't Stop, Won't Stop

Ask any NFL fan who the best quarterback of all time is and the unequivocal answer would be Tom Brady. It's common knowledge that Brady's NFL draft report was less than complimentary. He was described as: skinny, poor build, lacking ability and prone to getting knocked down early. None of these traits were considered close to the qualities of the high-octane sport of NFL, never mind in the key role of quarterback. In part due to this report, Brady could count himself lucky to be selected by the New England Patriots as the 199th pick in the sixth round of the

NFL draft, almost an afterthought amidst the fanfare of the draft day in the year 2000. No one, other than Tom Brady himself, would have believed that 23 years later he would be the 3x NFL MVP and won 7 Super Bowl's, making him the greatest quarterback of all time. Yet he took his chance when it came and made the most of his talent, worked on his ability and made sure that he left a legacy in the sport.

Tom Brady's incredible career could have been written off before it started if he had succumbed to a loss of confidence at the results of the less than complimentary NFL combine report and subsequent lowly draft pick. Instead, he saw an opportunity. He took initiative and made it happen. This is often the case in academy football. A player can be smaller, slower, weaker and less robust than their teammates in adolescence, yet given their maturation status, this is not to say they aren't talented enough. It is pertinent to say that in fact, those who don't physically develop as quickly as their peers may have a benefit in the long term by developing their technical ability to maintain their position within the academy system. This can also be the case with footballers in the professional game who fall out of favour, dropped or let go. If you remain confident and have the belief in your own ability, the chances are that you will get another opportunity and come back stronger for it. Don't let up and do believe in yourself.

I could quite easily have given up myself after being released by my home town club. I'd only ever wanted to be play as a professional for them and now, at 15, I'd been told I had no chance. It hurt, a lot. Yet a force inside me kept me on track to achieve my dream. I wasn't necessarily angry, but I did have a burning fire in my belly to prove the naysayers wrong and myself right. I was going to be a professional footballer, no matter what one coach said about his opinion of my ability. The sport is a fickle game and one that is oftentimes subjective to a single person's opinion, and no one is right 100% of the time. Don't let one negative outcome hold you back from a successful career. There will always be someone else just around the corner who will see the talent you have.

CHAPTER 7: BE COMFORTABLE BEING UNCOMFORTABLE

School heats up. GCSE's are around the corner and The Pro is being pulled back and forth between exams and life. He saunters through the season, foot off the gas with the contract in the bag. In April the chosen 9 scholars, young men with huge dreams and adequate ability, stand in their baggy suits at the stadium. A photo is taken of them all stood, smiling, the players and the coach, the guardian over their careers for the next two years. The photo, not quite boyband, not quite police line-up, is published in the local paper, matchday programme and club website. In the brief introductions of each of the new arrivals, The Pro is described as a 'composed, comfortable and strong defender, difficult to get past and able to pick out a pass'.

That same day, the players are introduced to their new families. They will each move into 'digs', foster families who provide a substitute home for the players from out of town. The Pro is placed in a nice suburban home a 30-minute walk to the stadium. They are given the move in date, 30th June. The same day as his last GCSE exam. His new family seem welcoming enough, and the move is made easier knowing that one of his teammates will be moving in too, a new brother to go with his new parents. His own parents seem to be happy with the whole situation and as a young man, this pacifies The Pro, even though the pangs of fear nibbled at him as he envisioned the huge shift his life was to make in a matter of months.

The school examination period starts in earnest in May. Training ceases as attention is turned to algebraic equations and the fundamentals of French. By the middle of the month, muscles are losing memory, fitness is faltering and exams remain incessant. The Pro hears his school friends planning parties for after their final exam, summer holidays, which college they're deciding to enrol in. One night during a lull in the exam period he goes to one of the friends' houses for a night playing FIFA. His friends drink alcopops, smoke cigarettes and cannabis, frolic in the free and easy weekend ahead. They turn from adolescence to early adulthood, experimenting and exploring. The Pro leaves. He can't risk inhaling the smoke from the weed, and feels isolated as his friends buzz on the sugary alcohol. He makes his excuses and departs into the darkness, jogging home to get some extra fitness work in. That evening signified the solidification of his difference, the juxtaposition as a social outcast and idol at the same time, moulding and morphing him into a bona fide Pro. He couldn't be sure of the emotions attached, both pride in his discipline and focus on the game he loved, as well as the fear of the isolation from the friends he grew up with.

The 30th June came around quick. He put on his school uniform for the last time, the pants flapping loose around his ankles as he hadoutgrown them months ago. Top button undone, tie lolling loosely, blazer slung over his shoulder. Meeting his friends on the walk to school, the same routine as every other school day throughout the last 5 years, a nervous nausea washed over him. This was the day. The last exam. The celebrations. The move. Schoolboy into the adult world.

Waving goodbye to his friends at the door, cheers of "Good Luck Pro", "Do us proud Pro", "We'll come and watch you soon!" and "Go on The Pro" rang out down the quiet road as his classmates swirled their school ties around their head, some wearing them like bandanas, youthful abandonment in full force. He smiled as he shut the front door, his suitcase laying packed by the bottom of the stairs, boots and shinpads, books and a PlayStation, clothes and snacks. Three hours later, the faithful car, the vehicle that defined his football to date, broke down on the motorway halfway to the digs he would now call home. Like an old cart horse flagging under the midday sun, the car simply stopped, engine smoking. Stood on the hard shoulder, waiting for the breakdown service, the family huddled together as the sun started its slow descent to the West, The Pro's suitcase at their feet, loaded with the next impending chapter of hopes and dreams. To the passing cars it would have made a notable family portrait, two adults and three children huddled together, all 5 of them on the precipice of change.

By 9pm, everyone somewhat bedraggled, the engine patched up and spluttering again as per usual, he hugs his family goodbye and they pile back into the car, an empty space now laying between his two siblings in the backseat. The old vehicle wheezes as it begins its journey back, winding its way down the suburban cul-de-sac, slowly fading to just a speck on the horizon until it turned right on to the main road towards the motorway, its indicators winking a good luck. The Pro cries. Hot tears. Frozen in a frame at the bedroom window that's shielded by the trees, he sits for a long period of time. That's it. The real deal. By 11pm his suitcase is unpacked, his new boots lined up by the door ready to go in the morning and his new roommate audibly sniffling away his own tears in the adjacent room.

Lesson 7: Be Comfortable Being Uncomfortable

Most footballers will know how relentless Sir Alex Ferguson was in his pursuit of silverware when he was manager of Manchester United. It is well documented that even after winning the Champions League in the most dramatic of fashions against Bayern Munich to complete the treble, that very evening he was setting targets for the following season. He didn't want his players nor himself to become complacent. Dwight Yorke, a star striker in the treble winning team, asked Ferguson for a season off as he had won all there was to win and was told in no uncertain terms why that wasn't happening. Ferguson wanted to win everything in his path and more often than not, he did. He wouldn't let anyone at the club become comfortable and reinvented the squad at least three times, letting key players go and replacing them with hungrier youngsters who wanted to win.

Leaving home to pursue a career at 16 is an uncomfortable reality of becoming a professional footballer and taking a different route from your friends is almost certainly the reality for many young players. To be comfortable doing so, you must be relentless in your pursuit of your dream, as Ferguson was in his desire to win games and trophies. Finding yourself in an unfamiliar environment can seem daunting at first, but it's essential that a footballer becomes comfortable being uncomfortable. Saying no to certain social events can be frustrating but being ready for training or a game means you're more likely to enjoy the fruits of your labour on the pitch. Football moves quickly, and it forgets even quicker. Don't let complacency hold you back.

I missed countless parties, holidays and family events whilst in hot pursuit of my dream. I was lucky that the people closest to me always supported my journey and didn't feel a need to question the decisions I was making, no matter how tough or strange they may have been. One particular weekend in between Christmas and New Year I stayed out past 1am when I had to be at training for 10am the next day. As soon as I stepped through the door - bearing in mind I hadn't touched any alcohol - my Mum read me the riot act and questioned my dedication to my football. Looking back now, I actually believe she might have been relieved that I'd been out with my schoolmates and let my hair down a little, but she was invested in my dream because she saw how happy football could make me and how hard I had worked to be in this position.

CHAPTER 8: SEASON'S CHANGE

The Pro is doubled over, gasping for breath, swallowing down the sick that's bubbling hot in his throat, a seismic amount waiting to spew from his guts. His pounding heart is punching through his new training kit, the clubs badge pulsing as though the material has come alive in a convulsion of sweat and shock.

"Get up! Get up now, you've got 12 seconds rest left, on your feet, keep moving!" bellows the youth team coach, a tall, silver haired former striker with a pedigree of producing professional players.

The Pro struggles to his feet, lolling in the searing sun and staggering to the start line, the image of a heavyweight boxer who should have stayed down for the count.

"Gooooooooooo….18 seconds to get there and back, don't be late. Gooooooooooooooooo…"

The Pro opens his stride across the freshly mown summer grass, a verdant green at the start of every pre-season before turning a dirty brown by the third or fourth heavy rainfall of September. Racing away from the new coach and his militant orders, The Pro and the rest of the first-year scholars turn sharply at the half way line and then race back to the touchline, fearing the worst if they fail to make the allocated time of 18 seconds.

"Threeeeee, Twoooooooooo, Onnnnneeeeeeeeeeeee…."

Dictates the man in the driving seat of his dreams for the next two years, his North East accent booming louder as he lifts his head from his stopwatch to see all of the nine new scholars still some 10 yards away from the touchline at which they should have arrived. The Pro collapses in a heap alongside the others, sure that the afternoons torture is over and that he can crawl back to his digs to sleep and recover.

"Not fit enough lads, not fit enough. Second years, you lads can go, if you're not coming back to the stadium, I'll see you tomorrow. First years, get up, one more set to do. You won't be playing for me like this, 6 more runs, let's go!"

The second years hug and cheer then jeer at the first years, smugness personified. The Pro is broken and now the coach demands one more set of 6 runs, the three sets prior not sufficing his sadistic quest for fitness from his squad. By the fourth run, 5 first years have vomited, 2 are splayed out on the floor making strange noises and all of them are questioning what they have signed up for. It's a tough start to life as a footballer for The Pro, one that isn't going to let up.

The next three months goes as follows:

Wake, shower, eat, walk to the stadium, get changed, prepare first team equipment, minibus to training ground, train, collect first team equipment, minibus back to stadium, shower, change, eat, clean changing rooms, walk home, eat, sleep.

Matchdays follow a similar and regular itinerary, although instead of training, The Pro is more often than not sat on the bench as the second-year players start games, their nous of the game seeing them automatically selected above the first year's naivety. In three months, The Pro starts 3 games, playing a meagre total of 280 minutes in 12 weeks. It wasn't much progress. In addition to playing, the youth team players must also attend college to continue their education 1 day a week. With 11 A* to B graded GCSE's, The Pro wants to study A Levels rather than a BTEC in Sport, which is the only course offered to the players. His Mum calls the club and enquires as to the possibility of The Pro doing A Levels instead, to which the answer from the club is curt and straight to the point,

"What do you want him to be love? A student, or a footballer?"

"I don't see why he can't be both?" counters his Mum.

"There isn't the time, he has to be focused on football only right now."

That is the final answer and his strong academic aptitude all but disappears in order to assimilate with his peers. Aged 16 and in back-to-back classes with other young footballers, most of whom are more interested in literally anything other than the assignments, The Pro falls in line with the pack and begins to resent every minute spent in the college's stuffy walls. He spends most of the time staring out of the window, sometimes daydreaming of playing in the first team, wondering what he needs to do to get there, other times wishing he was at home with his friends, the same as any other teenager. He learns very little.

After 4 months, a devastating piece of news tears The Pro's teenage world apart and sends him into a tailspin. On dark and wet October evening, one of The Pro's schoolfriends dies in a car crash in his hometown. Another friend travelling in the same car lays in a coma for over three weeks, fighting for his life wired to machines. The impact of such a terribly sad incident ripples through the entire community. He goes home immediately to be with his friends and family. For The Pro, football can wait.

Football, however, never waits. There is no professional help from the club, no counsellor, no therapy, no one to talk to amongst the pseudo machoism in the changing rooms and out on the pitch. The Pro goes back to the digs and feels lonelier than ever, forced to process the sudden death of a friend, and the possible imminent death of another, in a small bedroom, miles away from home or any of his support network. The reality of chasing his dream punches him in the face with force, bottled up emotions tightening their grip on his broken heart. His footballing development is hampered, a few weeks on the bench with limited game time and then extra afternoon sessions with the physio to catch up on fitness. There was no time for sentiment in the ruthless search for success.

Before Christmas, turmoil ensues again. He is still not playing regular football. His friends are processing the loss of their mate together in his hometown, gradually finding their way again, their normality, sharing new experiences as a unit. The Pro is called into the club secretary's office, a short haired, fiery but friendly lady who ran a tight ship at the club.

"Sit down Rory, make yourself comfy. How's everything going?"

"Yeah, ok I suppose, I'm good" replied The Pro, nervously scanning the small, cluttered office filled with coffee-stained paperwork and old football memorabilia.

"Ok, well, we've some news for you, do you want the good or the bad?" asks the secretary quizzically.

"Erm…either I suppose" responds The Pro, his stomach dropping then twisting into a thousand knots. His head turns into an F1 track, thoughts speeding through his brain at speed; Is everyone OK at home? Is he in trouble? Has he done something wrong? Is his contract going to be terminated? Zooming through his head at breakneck speed.

"OK, let's get the bad news out of the way, and don't look so worried" pacifies the secretary, her tone suggesting the news wasn't about to be life changing.

But it was.

"So, the family you've been staying with have asked that you and your teammate move out, as soon as possible. They don't want to have two teenagers in their house anymore and there's not a lot we can do. They've no complaints about either of you, it's just the way it goes sometimes... well... rarely" she states matter of fact, looking for a reaction.

The Pro furrows his brow and takes a deep breath. Well, it's not the worst news in the world, but it's not ideal.

"Nothing we can do to stay? Shall I speak to them?" enquires The Pro.

"Their minds made up love, they want you out this weekend, signed the paperwork, it's all done and dusted. So, onto the good news. We've sorted you out with a new place, it's over in a different part of town but you'll be OK there, the family's been doing this for years, and the goalkeepers already there so you'll settle quick."

And just like that, The Pro took another, albeit different, form of rejection on the chin, bottled it up in the recess of his mind and a week later was sat in his new bedroom, the cold winter draught blowing through the cracked glass in the window, the dark wallpaper on the four walls closing in on him.

"Oi, I'm going out, have a drive and a quick smoke, wanna come?" asks the goalkeeper, barging into The Pro's room as if he owns it. The goalkeeper, who has just passed his driving licence, keeps a pack of 20 cigarettes next to a bottle of aftershave in the glove box of his Vauxhall Corsa.

"Nah, I'm alright mate, cheers" responds The Pro, not wanting to go out driving all night after what had happened to his friend more than not wanting to smoke. But he didn't want to do that either.

"Alright mate, inabit" disappears the keeper.

At Christmas the players are given two weeks off to be with their family. Before they go, the coach assesses their fitness levels. They are required to run up and down every step in the 20000-capacity stadium. After that they head inside to the sports hall to complete a Bleep Test. Then they're back outside for some short and sharp repeated sprints. It's a hellish day.

"You'll earn this break lads!" bellows the coach as they try their best to sprint on empty tanks through the thick mud.

The same afternoon, showered and barely able to stand, the players return home for a much-needed break. Over the Christmas period away from the club, one teammate is arrested for joyriding, two are called back to train with the first team and one doesn't return back to the club again, home being too much of a pull against his dream. The Pro spends quality time with his family and friends, recharged and ready to go for the second half of the season. January comes and goes, fitness is rebuilt, he sits on the bench more often than plays.

In January, he is offered to move into new digs, this time sharing with an older, loving couple and a second-year player who had not only just broken into the first team at the club but also the senior Welsh national team too. From the first minute, he feels more at home than he ever has since arriving in this new town. The new found stability transfers to his contentment at the club. He goes home each day and talks at length to the other player at the dinner table, asking him what it's like in the first team, how he got there, what he himself can do to improve and break through as well. The second-year, a mature head on young shoulders, mentors The Pro. He starts to thrive, cementing a spot in the starting line-up for the youth team and breaking into the reserve team too. For the first time, it feels good to be chasing his dream.

In February, his knee cartilage rips in a training ground tackle. Two trips to a specialist confirm that although it's not a serious injury, it requires keyhole surgery. Two more trips to the hospital come and go, including one to the surgeon for the operation itself. He's running again four days post op. Unfortunately for The Pro, it leaves only 3 games of the season left. The youth team win the regional league at a canter, the reserves the same. The Pro can't get back into the team. He watches from the side-lines as his teammates win the Cup too. It's at this point The Pro realises that football is an individual game hidden within a team sport. Lifting the Cup is bittersweet. But he has a glimmer of burning desire for his second year, it just needs to be ignited.

Lesson 8: Season's Change

Every year, in most places on Earth, the season's change four times. Winter, with its cold, bleak climate blossoms into spring, a time of growth, hope and new life. By the time summer comes along, with its long, bright, hot days, adventure and revelry is never too far away, before autumn arrives with its vivid colours, colder nights and harvesting of food for the inevitable winter on the horizon. These cyclical seasonal changes each have their positive and negative attributes, with some people enjoying cosy winter nights and others the reliably hot summers spent outdoors.

As with football seasons, the cycles of change are inevitable. Some years, a particularly harsh winter may last longer than expected, or a beautiful summer could extend longer than usual too. Football seasons also ebb and flow and have a degree of unpredictability about them. For each player, form will come and go, their team's performances may blow hot and cold and they will face numerous challenge such as injuries and not being selected. I experienced all of the above in my first full time year in professional football. It was a steep learning curve, fraught with difficulties but also many great times and good memories, much like any calendar year with four seasons.

As a footballer, you have to take the rain with the shine, the storms with the sun and the snow with the sand. What is always certain however is that a season has a fixed number of games, that opportunities must be taken when offered and that contracts inevitably will come to an end. To be able to control your own mindset with a positive perspective is the key to maintaining a chance of success as a footballer, whatever a season may throw at you.

CHAPTER 9: FINDING YOUR PLACE

The ignition The Pro needed comes in a far flung South Asian outpost, in a post season tour. Yet the flame ignited is a new one. The town in which the club The Pro plays for has a large Bangladeshi community. Racial tension had dominated the town for years and in an effort to increase harmony within the local community, the club had been invited to tour Bangladesh in the off season on a three-game tour.

On an astoundingly sweaty, sweltering hot day in Dhaka, Bangladesh, the touring football club is greeted at the international airport by throngs of ecstatic fans, thousands of faces crowding the public areas of the arrivals area, hundreds clambering over fences for a closer glimpse of the football team from England. The paparazzi, their official lanyards worn around their necks with discernible pride, buzz around the players faces snapping away, whilst the TV cameras follow them closely. News reporters hustle and bustle each other out of the way with elbows and microphones to be the first to ask a question to these superstars in their midst. It's an overwhelming experience for the jetlagged lads, one that The Pro doesn't find comfortable at first, but begins to enjoy quickly. The squad and coaches assemble on the arrival stairwell, with the ex-SAS security detail that's in tow with them hovering menacingly in the background, eyes constantly scanning the ever-changing scene to perceive any potential threats.

Three days in to the 10-day tour, The Pro starts the first tour game against the reigning Bangladeshi league champions. It's another hot, humid and hectic day. The stadium fills with anticipation from the Bangladeshi fans, eager to see how their players stand up against an English team. The answer is a draw. The game is dominated not by the four goals in a 2-2 draw however, but in the frequent aggressive incidents that result in The Pro and his team departing the stadium via a back exit, still in their match kit and unshowered, before a riot broke out amongst the hostile and baying crowd. The fervour of the game had got to the hosts, who had their team bolstered by 4 wily and antagonistic Argentinians who spat, punched and kicked off the ball at every opportunity. The Pro's fellow centre back took offence after he had been spat on for the second time and all hell broke loose. A 22-man brawl erupted, the players and staff on the side-line scuffled before calm was restored. The security detail pulled the plug on the whole thing as soon as the final whistle blew 10 minutes later. So much for community relations.

The adrenaline was still racing through The Pro as the team ran onto the team bus, encouraged to pick up the pace by the burly ex-SAS men, a sour scent of sweat permeating the aisle when all players and staff were safely aboard. As the bus lurched out of the hulking stadium onto the packed and crowded streets, some players were happy to be safely on the bus, others were baying for the blood of the opposition, and the rest sat in a daze having experienced danger on the football pitch for the first time. The Pro looked out of the window at all the colourful lights, the deafening sounds, the staring faces, the street vendors pedalling their wares, the packed pavements, the strange smells overpowering the sweat inside the bus. He felt exhilarated. A man on a pushbike pulled up alongside the bus, smiling and waving. With an old Arsenal shirt on, it was obvious he had been at the game. As the bus found some space and got into second gear out of the traffic, the man fervently pedalled to keep up. He continued to wave, smiling and weaving his way behind the bus through heavy traffic and onto the highway all the way back to the team hotel over 7km away, never losing sight of the bus. Football was bigger than the country and leagues The Pro had grown up in- it was a game beloved across the globe.

Two more games against the Bangladeshi national team saw the tour to come to a relentlessly exciting end. There were private chartered flights into obscure military bases, police escorts through the streets of slums and cities, days relaxing at the British embassy pool and no end of fun amongst the players and staff, including a final night when everyone was invited to have a few drinks in the hotel bar with the enthusiastic hotel staff. It was an amazing adventure.

Lesson 9: Finding Your Place

There is a TV show called Race Around The World which pits 6 teams of 2 against each other in an exciting adventure format. The show requires each pair of travellers to get from one side of the world to the other without flying, on a budget that is the same cost as a flight and through various checkpoints which add an element of competition. It is a fantastic reality show, complete with the inevitable drama but also the nuances of teamwork, fatigue, frustration and pure joy thrown in for good measure. It reminded me of the challenges a footballer faces for many reasons, as well as showing just how amazing the world is and how many opportunities exist out there for those willing to step out of their comfort zone.

As a footballer, the world can seem quite a small place and time a vacuum. You're often focused entirely on the next game, the next training session, the next pass. Your decisions are based around the immediate future and not the bigger picture. Race Around The World follows suit, with contestants forced to make quick decisions and to make the best choice available to them in that moment. However, there is an end goal and the need to keep within a budget means a longer-term view is also essential to success. This is an unpopular view I highly encourage every footballer to take on board. One day, your career will end. That will hopefully be through your own autonomy, but as we know, the statistics suggest that being released is often the reason a football career is terminated. How do you budget for your future beyond football and your current contract?

The world is full of endless possibilities, adventure and growth. Football is the world's most popular sport. Add the two up and you can see you fairly quickly that there is more than your immediate environment in which football is played. Just like the Argentinian players in Bangladesh, if you are willing to step outside of your familiar environment there is playing opportunities around the whole world, complete with new experiences, cultures and friendships. Don't be too quick to write off your potential because your current environment doesn't fit right now - find a place where you're valued.

CHAPTER 10: FORM IS TEMPORARY, CLASS IS PERMANENT

By December of his second and final contracted year at the club, The Pro was playing poorly, doubting his love of the game and struggling to find any form in training or matches at youth or reserve team level. Then came the pre requisite FA Level 2 Coaching Licence course run by the governing bodies to give youth team players alternative routes in the game if they didn't continue playing, which many didn't. The majority of the players had an indignant attitude to education and courses such as these, The Pro being no different on day 1. By the end of the course, he had regained not only his love for the game, but also his confidence. He excelled as a coach, enjoying being creative and helping the young players he coached become better through drill development. He passed the course with flying colours, whilst on the pitch his form picked up exponentially. He was moved to right back and found the relative freedom of the position liberating. Before long he was starting at right back for the reserves each week and pushing to train with the first team on a regular basis.

Like a horse emerging from the back of the pack to storm to a comfortable win, The Pro kept up this unwavering momentum and became a leading player in each game. On a Friday in March, he was walking with two of his teammates back to their digs when his phone buzzed in his pocket. The youth team Coach's name flashed up. The Pro's stomach dropped once again, what had he forgot to do, what mistake had he made this time?

"Have you got a suit son?" asked the Coach

"Ermm, no, I don't think so Coach…"

"Well, you better get over to Next and buy one then, you're with the first team tomorrow" instructed the Coach.

"Are you being serious?" asked The Pro, incredulous at what he had just heard.

"The gaffers told me to tell you to report at 1.15pm at the ground, in your suit, you'll be on the bench but be ready. Well done son, see you tomorrow!" and with that the coach hung up the phone, leaving The Pro stood on the pavement grinning from ear to ear, weak at the knees with excitement and nervous energy. He told his teammates, who were good friends and happy for him despite a hint of natural resentment apparent in their eyes.

He walked with them back to their digs, his being the furthest away at the opposite end of town, the other side of a large graveyard. He sprinted through the graveyard even faster than usual, this time for reasons of elation rather than being purely petrified. When he got to his room he texts his Dad, "call me", then waited for the call.

"Hi Dad, you got a minute?"

"Yeah mate, is all OK?" asked his Dad.

"Not really, the Coach just phoned me then after training. I'm not playing tomorrow morning" sighed The Pro with feigned disappointment.

"Oh, why? That's weird, you've been playing well too..." questioned his Dad.

"Yeah, I know. But I've to get a suit he said." Deadpanned The Pro.

"A suit? Why? Have you not got one? What for?" shot back his Dad.

"I'm only on the bench for the first team tomorrow, that's why!" exclaimed The Pro.

" F***ING GET IN THERE, WELL DONE! That's amazing, proud of you, who are they playing?" his excited Dad celebrated.

"Huddersfield at home, should be a good game!" answered The Pro.

One suit, one day later and The Pro walks into the changing room to see him matchday shirt hanging up on a peg, Winters above the number 39 printed on the back of the shirt, pride electrifying him. He warms up with the squad as the stadium begins to fill, the fans chanting as the pre-game anticipation built up. Two hours later and it's all over. He doesn't get on the pitch but it's an incredible experience to be involved in an official league game with a packed stadium and 3 points on the line. A taste of what he wants. A recognition of his form and potential. An official matchday shirt with his name and number on it. Two weeks later he makes the bench again, away at Swindon Town, then again at home to Leyton Orient the week after. This takes the season into its final month, with contract decision day looming on the horizon.

The day before contract decisions are made, The Pro lines up for his club against Manchester United in the Manchester Senior Cup Final, playing right back against Danny Wellbeck on the left for United in a team containing players who would go on to be full internationals and Premier League regulars. After 60 minutes, Wellbeck is substituted off, unable to make much headway against The Pro. After the game, a 2-2 draw, The Pro sees his Dad for a quick chat before heading back to his digs to try to get some sleep before the big morning the following day.

"Should be good tomorrow mate, well played tonight too, you looked class,"

"Yeah, I reckon I've got a chance eh, I'll ring you as soon as I know" said The Pro, quietly confident in his chances of signing a pro deal the next day.

Lesson 10: Form is Temporary, Class is Permanent

The golfer Brooks Koepka starred, somewhat unflatteringly, in the revealing docuseries Full Swing. Suffering a terrible loss in form, Koepka is dramatically depicted as the man who had it all and is on the verge of losing it all. As he struggles to regain his form, the show paints him as a lonely, sad figure, struggling to connect with his wife at home and his own frustrations bubbling to the surface. It's a real time picture of professional sport. His own swing, the very skill that gave him Major title wins was, all of a sudden, failing him.

Fast forward a year and Koepka has joined an elite band of golfers to win 5 major tournament's, as well as becoming the first LIV affiliated golfer to win a major tournament too. He's breaking new ground in the sport. Despite the dramatization that was inevitably provided by the show, Koepka is proof that form is temporary but class is permanent. To be able to reach the top of any field, there will be times along the way that you will lose form, hit a bump in the road and have a level of self-doubt that may feel debilitating. The understanding that this is only a temporary blip is essential to moving forwards quicker. It's too easy to say get your head down and crack on, yet an awareness of why you are suffering a loss of form may well be beneficial in accepting that it can be turned back around.

At the midway point of the second year of my contract, I was struggling for form. I couldn't seem to find any consistency in my performances and as the weeks rolled by, I applied increasing pressure on myself to play better. At first though, I blamed others. The coach's tactics, my teammate's ability, the state of the pitches, the inclement weather, anything but analysing my own flaws. It was the eventual acceptance of my poor form, and the looming contract decision day, that meant I sought the advice of the coach. Consequently, I applied his advice to implement the advanced skill of reflective practice to investigate why my form was suffering. It was a deep dive into maturing as a man and a football player. A change in position helped my cause in surging beyond my peers into the first team squad, yet my continued uplift in form was ultimately assisted by my methodical analysis of my strengths and weaknesses, as suggested by the coach, on a daily basis.

CHAPTER 11: REFRAME REJECTION

Less than 24 hours after playing against Manchester United, The Pro is summoned to the boardroom. The gaffer and the Youth Team Coach are sat behind an old, mahogany table that dominated the room, facing a single empty seat. The set up was even more ominous than any dentist's office he had ever seen. He sat down, shuffling with nerves in his seat, as the single yellow form appeared in the youth coach's hand and was pushed over to The Pro, radiating like an apocalyptic supernova.

"OK Rory, we'll get straight to the point son. We're not offering you a professional deal…."

The room began to spin, The Pro experiencing a new form of vertigo he had not known prior to the Gaffers opening sentence. He tried to focus on the yellow form. It moved closer, pushed towards him by an indistinct hand, as a pen suddenly appearing alongside the sheet.

"No reserves next year…not ready for men's football…don't need defenders…help you…sign here…"

snippets of distinguishable words dash in and out of his hearing. His head continues to spin, blurred vision and a rising feeling of nausea enveloping him. He scribbles a signature; the same one he's been used to signing on the clubs' shirts for fans and in matchday programmes. It's done, he's been let go. He calls his Dad, telling him he's been released in a state of sad disbelief.

"Hi Dad…"

"Alright mate, how did it go?" a hopeful and positive tone to his Dad's reply.

"I didn't get one Dad, they've let me go.." came The Pro's despondent reply.

"And you need another suit too?" laughed his Dad, reversing The Pro's first team call up prank.

"No Dad, they've let me go, they've released all of us other than the keeper. I'm done. Can't believe it" emotion straining The Pro's voice. He stands shellshocked in the away team dugout at the stadium. Shivering in the shade of the main stand behind him.

"Oh mate, that's shit. I can't understand that. How are you? Keep your head up, I'll drive up with your Mum later on, what are you all doing now?" rattles off his Dad, sadness now dominating his tone.

When the released players had all gathered their thoughts and emotions, made the phone calls and wiped the tears and punched the wall and sat in the changing room staring into space and commiserated and hugged and laughed because they didn't want to cry in front of each other, after all that's done, the players go to the nearby Pizza Hut. 8 of the 9 of them with their worlds cataclysmically changed as they push stuffed crust pizza around their plates. The keeper who got a pro deal is sheepish. He is the least professional of them all but he has had a slice of good fortune. Sometimes that's all there is to it.

2 days after playing against Manchester United, The Pro is at home, silently eating a roast dinner and listening to his family try to raise his spirits, sounding like a distant static as his head replays the comments made by the gaffer and the youth team coach about his release. The despair is intolerable. He goes to bed, cries into his pillow. Struggles to sleep.

3 days after playing against Manchester United, The Pro returns to his digs after two days at home. He is met with sympathy from his professional roommate and the digs family. He goes to his room, sad, angry, confused and at a loss as to what to do next.

4 days after playing against Manchester United, The Pro lines up for the reserves for the last time against Leicester City. The reserve team coach tells them this is a shop window opportunity for them, a chance to impress scouts in the stadium. The team lose 8-2, with a discernible lack of commitment or confidence amongst the squad, 9 of whom had been released 3 days earlier and had no support from the club since.

5 days after playing against Manchester United, the reserve team coach gathers all the released players and berates them for a lack of professionalism the night before. He tells them this is why they didn't deserve professional

contracts, why they won't get another club and why they don't deserve to be at the club any longer. The Pro sits and listens. The words burn his soul.

7 days after playing against Manchester United, The Pro plays his last game for the club, a dead rubber youth team game in which he goes through the motions and is substituted off for a 15-year-old with 20 minutes remaining. He throws his shirt off in despair, gets changed and drives back to his digs, crying.

8 days after playing against Manchester United, The Pro, in a fit on unbridled anger and rage, punches a hole through his laptop screen after he reads about his release on the club website. One name amongst a list of 18 first team and youth players released. One name amongst the hundreds of players released up and down the country at the end of the season.

10 days after playing against Manchester United, The Pro watches Danny Wellbeck, the player he marked out of that very game, make his debut for Manchester United in the Premier League.

14 days after playing against Manchester United, The Pro is moving back into his family home from his digs, driving his battered old VW Polo back on the motorway with all of his belongings, memories and broken dreams to his old bedroom he shares with his younger brother.

21 days after playing against Manchester United, The Pro is pulling down his cap in shame at his hometown McDonalds. The apron tied tight against his body, his footballers frame slouching to become unrecognisable. His

old schoolmate recognises him. Within 21 days it feels like the whole of his hometown knows of his demise. He has nowhere to hide.

Lesson 11: Reframe Rejection

Rejection has many faces, all of which seem truly awful at first glance. However, changing the perspective through which you view rejection can change not just the view of the past, but also your future. I have a close friend who had the expectation of becoming a Doctor thrust upon him by his family at a young age. His older siblings were in Medical School by the time we reached secondary school and, given his own academic strength, it seemed inevitable he would follow their path. At 18, he was rejected at the interview stage by each of the medical schools he had applied to. When I met up with him to commiserate, he was wearing a wide smile on his face and looked like the weight of the world had lifted from his shoulders. He was free from expectation and rather than feeling aggrieved by the apparent rejection, he was enraptured by the new possibilities that now lay ahead of him. His literal words were,

"I've not been rejected; I've been set free!"

At the time, I too had just been rejected by the football club I'd spent two years at. It wasn't the first time, given my hometown club had rejected me two years earlier. However, it didn't make the experience any easier. I was angry, confused, ashamed and lost. My outlook was negative and entirely different from my friend who had felt his burden lift. In contrast, I'd picked up the world from my friend's shoulders and put it on my own, which already felt too heavy to bear.

Rejection is never easy, particularly when the dream was your own and not someone else's that you were fulfilling. Finding another angle of framing the situation is imperative for a more successful recovery. You might have been released, but that's from one club, one set of opinions, one coach's decision. It's not a reflection of your ability, your potential or of your self-worth and identity. It's simply not the right place for you. Having someone to rationalise this for you is priceless in what can feel akin to a grieving process. The quicker you can accept the decision, with the right support, the quicker you can build a new chapter.

CHAPTER 12: IT'S LONELY AT THE TOP

The Pro gets the job at McDonalds because his parents aren't willing to allow him time to sulk and fall into a state of hubris.

"You're 18 now, if you're living here, you're contributing to the house, so you'll have to go and get a job" they chime.

He hates it at McDonalds. The smell. The shame. The reality of his situation.

He sends a letter to every one of the professional football clubs in England and Scotland once again, detailing his availability and willingness to trial during pre-season. This time, he doesn't get a single reply. He instead goes to local non-league clubs, with a naïve arrogance that he should still be a professional. Within 6 weeks of pre-season, he is signed by Fleetwood Town, a growing force in the non-league game, but he fails to make the first team squad when the season starts and has quit by the end of August.

His resilience has wavered, his confidence is shot and his football career is floating downriver.

The Pro has no love or desire left for the game. A call comes in from a University in America, offering him a partially funded scholarship on their soccer programme. His parents sit down with him and do the maths. Even with the partial funding, the family can't afford it. The US isn't a feasible option. The Pro now sees that even further education is a costly business and out of reach.

A call from his Mum to a teaching friend leads to The Pro sitting in the office of the local college, the same college most of his friends have just completed two years of studying their A Levels at, partying and socialising before starting university that September. The Pro listens to the Principle of the college tell him he has a place, and then is passed on to the college's football coach, who is ludicrously telling him he will help him become a professional again. The Pro walks out feeling conflicted. Here he is, 2 years behind his friends and peers, enrolling in a college and classes with his friends younger siblings who he's always seen as little kids. 2 years spent in the professional football world to end up back where he could have been 2 years previously. 2 years wasted. 2 years down the drain.

By the second week of the college term, he realises that the college coach means business. He is a strict disciplinarian. A former professional who played under Brian Clough at Nottingham Forest in an illustrious career, the coach's methods are somewhat bizarre- but they work. The Pro is managed and mentored brilliantly. He has a weekly one on one meeting with the coach which not only highlights his footballing strengths and weaknesses but focuses in on his mindset, his social life and his balance between football and his studies. It keeps The Pro accountable when it would have been easy to drift into the abyss. Extra training after regular sessions to maintain The Pro's fitness levels are commonplace and The Pro is singled out in team talks to the rest of the team as a standard bearer for the consistency required from them all as a collective. The Pro is buoyed by confidence and he rekindles his love for the game. Being the star player also suits him, with less pressure outside of the vacuum that is professional football and more pleasure attached to training, games and development. The educational side of the college also stimulates The Pro more than sitting in his room in digs playing on a PlayStation ever did. He enrols in English, History, Business and Media. He starts to feel the stress deflate and energy come back.

He quits McDonalds the same week that he makes the final cut for the England College's trials in early November. Using the weekend at Lilleshall for the final trial process as an excuse, he hands in his resignation and with that no more McNuggets will be dished out by him. It feels good to take off the cap and apron for the last time as he rushes out of the door, the stench of gherkins and mustard fading as he got further and further away.

Lilleshall is a different beast. The best 30 players in the country's college system line up to do battle for a place in an 18-man squad that will represent England in an international tournament in Italy the following February. It's a long weekend, constantly being monitored and observed, judged and assessed. The Pro thrives in most of the drills and activities. He's used to the process, being judged by coaches since he was 8 years old. On the Sunday the final game is played. He is centre back and is up against the star of the whole process, a Ghanaian striker from the Right to Dream programme in England on a football scholarship. He is fast, strong, direct and a clinical finisher. The Pro knows it's a test set up by the coaching team to see how he copes. He manages the striker with aplomb. A clean sheet and not a sniff for the striker. He's selected for England Colleges. On the drive back home in the college minibus his coach, and mentor, asks The Pro to reflect upon the last 6 months. It's been a strange journey.

"Well, I was playing against Man United 6 months ago.." recollects The Pro.

"Yeah son, you were. And now you're playing for England!" beams back the mentor.

"Yeeessssssssss!" celebrate The Pro and the mentor in unison.

Lesson 12: It's Lonely At The Top

As young boy, football dominated my thoughts and was my main hobby. There were other trends which came and went though. One of those which seemed to gain immense popularity was WWE wrestling, the sheer drama and athletic prowess of these American monsters was appealing to impressionable youngsters who loved the show. One of the superstars of this era of wrestling is a well- known actor today, Dwayne Johnson, formerly known as The Rock. With his trademark raised eyebrow and sculpted physique, he was one of the more popular wrestlers and seemed indestructible. He was put upon the same pedestal as the Premier League players by me and my friends. Yet all I saw was his posturing and confidence. I didn't know about The Rock beyond the character he played in the ring.

Recently I came across an article that detailed Dwayne Johnson's journey. It surprised me to find out that he had aspired to be an NFL player and had got very close after committing his adolescence to the sport. Ultimately though, The Rock became an icon in WWE because Dwayne was rejected by American Football. Having been let go by Canadian team Calgary Stampeder's, he moved back home where his family made a living from wrestling. Johnson felt like a failure from football and fell into a state of depression before finding a mentor, Pat Patterson. He shifted through the gears of Pat's famous work ethic and discipline to emerge as a leading light of professional wrestling. It's no surprise to now see him as a Hollywood A lister and inspiration to many for his mindset and attitude in the face of adversity, yet his rewiring and resilience is often talked about in the same breath as the importance of the mentorship provided by Pat Patterson.

Dwayne Johnson's story is the ultimate in stepping up after rejection. It is easy to see the similarities between The Rock's journey and my own journey in football, as well as that of my teammates too. I had dedicated 7 years to one football club, the team I supported, the team I dreamt about playing for every night, the team that was developing me into a professional football player. The abruptness of my release, the cold justification used to validate the decision and the lack of after care in place left me bereft. Without a supportive family and an unbiased, supportive mentor, I may have never got back on the path after such a direct hit.

CHAPTER 13: GET BACK UP!

As God Save the Queen blasts out of the Rome stadium, The Pro lines up in the pristine white Three Lions shirt, tingles running down his spine as he is about to represent his country, England, on the international stage. They say representing one's own country is the highest honour an athlete can achieve, and at this moment in time The Pro would definitely agree. As the national anthem continues with all of it's pomp and ceremony through the stadium's soundsystem, the opposition for the group stage game, Latvia, stand in silence. The Pro also remains silent, in quiet contemplation of how meteoric his rise, from McDonalds to England, has been in the last 6 months. He thinks of his mentor and the words of wisdom he had shared before The Pro had joined the rest of the squad to fly to Rome from Bristol airport.

"Hey, you. Look at me. You deserve this, you've worked your balls off for this opportunity, your whole life, coming back to college when you could have gone off the rails. Playing for the college team every week when you're good enough to be in the football league. Son, believe in yourself out there, you deserve to be there. And you know what else? Bloody *enjoy* it, get a smile on your face, you're playing for your country man!"

The encouraging words echo through his headspace as he slowly lifts his head and grins, breaking into a huge ear to ear smile as the anthem comes to a crescendo and the two teams move to shake each other's hands. The game itself results in a comfortable win, a solid 90 minutes for The Pro snuffing out any danger from the big Latvian strikers. The Pro solidifies his starting place as the team win the group with ease, progressing to a semi-final against Lithuania before the prospect of the hosts Italy waiting in the final at the national stadium in Rome. They beat Lithuania on penalties, a tense, tight affair that is played on The Pro's 19th birthday. It was a year to the day since he had been playing in the reserves for his former club. The Pro was on a path he didn't know existed a year earlier, one that wasn't offered to him by anyone. It was forged himself, the travails of a young footballer, gilded through a fortitude built on resilience and overcoming adversity, assisted by his family and his mentor, attained by his perseverance and ultimately, his belief in his own ability.

The tournament's final is a less a spectacle of fantastic football but more a lesson in gamesmanship and match intelligence. The Italian hosts go 1-0 up in the 20th minute and spend the next 70+ minutes of the game executing a near perfect game plan, frustrating their English opponents via both patient possession and a rather cruder, more cynical side of the game with time wasting and simulation. The Pro is as frustrated as every other English player on the pitch as the final whistle blows and the Italians celebrate their victory riotously. He is also fascinated by the way the opposition were so tactically advanced in comparison to the English, winning the tournament with a ruthless proficiency. He feels like he learns more in those battling 90 minutes than in much of the first year of his youth team scholarship. The Pro takes these lessons back to England and to the exciting news that his performances have earnt him trials at League One and League Two clubs.

He goes into train and play in reserve games at Stockport County, Accrington Stanley, Rochdale and Morecambe FC. He finds his form at Morecambe, training every day with the first team, playing for the reserves each week and trying his best to balance it all with his college studies. A phone call in March to his Mum from a college tutor questions The Pro's attendance at college the last two months. He gets a lecture from his Mum that evening.

"Rory, your attendance is shocking. You know how fickle football is, you've got to stay on top of your college work too" sensibly suggested his Mum

"Mum, I'm going in, I'm getting the grades. But not everyone will understand this journey I'm on, they could never dream this big themselves, or take the knocks I've had and keep going. It's easy to stand over me criticising but until he's stepped in my shoes, he can't ever understand why I'm missing some mornings" replied The Pro.

“Please remember the nature of it all Rory is all I’m saying, you’re 19 so I won’t tell you what to do, I’m only looking out for you” empathised his Mum.

He embraces her in a big hug, thankful for the unwavering support his family have given him despite the tumultuous journey it had been up to that point.

The next day at college, the coach and the tutor sit down with The Pro. The coach listens intently to the tutor as he outlines why The Pro is in danger of falling behind with his academics. The coach cuts in as the tutor begins to lambast The Pro,

“Both of you, listen to me. College is important, qualifications will stand the test of time and set him up for the path to university and beyond” says the coach, glaring at The Pro.

The Pro averts his gaze, looking to the floor, disappointed that he has let his mentor down.

“And, he knows that full well” states the coach, this time meeting the tutors gaze, “He’s got a second chance right now to go and live every boy's dream, yours at one point too most likely, and he’s damn close to achieving it. He’ll pass his exams; he’s a bright boy and I’m watching him like a hawk. But let me tell you this. When he’s training, he’s training. His dream right now isn’t to go to university, it’s to be a professional footballer and there ’s 0.0001% who get there. He’s so close, support him, don’t shoot him down please!”

The tutor sits back, inhales deeply and looks at The Pro.

"OK. Good luck mate, I'm excited to see you play!" exclaims the tutor.

The coach shoots a knowing wink at The Pro and walks out of the office, leaving The Pro to say his goodbyes to the tutor on his own. He walks out of the office 5 seconds later 10 feet tall. The priceless value of a mentor, unbiased and fully supportive of his dreams, resonated with him yet again.

3 weeks after the meeting with the tutor, The Pro is A Pro. A one-year professional contract is offered to him by Morecambe for the next season, with the potential he has shown giving him a realistic chance of breaking into the first team. Supporting this belief is the presence of a former teammate from his academy days at his hometown club, who, released at 14, is now a regular starter for the first team at Morecambe and scoring goals in League Two.

The pride he has when signing the dotted line on his contract is evident in the confidence he now carries in himself, in his football, in his AS Level exams and in his summer break in Greece. The pride he has in finally 'making it' as a professional, amongst the millions of young boys who dream of attaining such a feat, of the thousands who are attached to professional clubs from the age of 8, to the hundreds who are offered youth team contracts each year, to the finite few who do actually sign a pro deal. The years of dedication to the sport, of silent graft in the alleyway, of constant sacrifice, of mile after mile in the family's old car, of rejection and despair, ups and downs and round and rounds. All culminating in inking the signature on the contract. The Pro is A Pro! The year is capped off by the college's awards night. The Pro is the recipient of Sportsperson of the Year, a proud moment as it is, but one that leaves tears in The Pro's eyes as he collects the trophy, named in memory of his friend who passed away in the car crash just 3 years before. It is a fitting end to a brilliant year.

Lesson 13: Get Back Up

In 2018, during the twelfth and final round of the WBC World Heavyweight Championship against the fierce Deontay Wilder in Los Angeles, the giant Tyson Fury was knocked down to the canvas by his opponent. It looked like the fight was over. Fury's 6ft 10inch frame was splayed out on the rings floor, eyes closed and as the referees 10 second count got to five, Fury was still out cold. 4 seconds later, he was back on his feet and ready to go again. When questioned how he managed to get back up and continue to go toe to toe and secure a draw in the fight, he out it down to two factors. One was his faith, the other was his innate fighting spirit and a never say die attitude.

A football career will contain many moments equivalent to Fury's knock down and seemingly miraculous resurrection. The boxing champions words can bring a deeper insight into my own journey, and perhaps to any footballers in fact. Take Faith as an example. My faith in my own ability was encouraged, nurtured and supported by my family and by my mentor. Without their support, I may never have got off the canvas. It was the same with my innate fighting spirit, which at times I forgot I possessed, until it was coaxed out of me once again by my mentor who would not allow me to give up. That never say die attitude, which every elite sportsperson has to some extent, had to be guided correctly by someone who had lived that journey themselves. I had dreams, but after so many rejections, I couldn't make myself believe them. Having a mentor resulted in some hard truths being doled out to me, whilst also reinstating the belief I had in my own ability to make my ambition my reality. Having this support, rooted in care, was priceless in my journey from Manchester United to McDonalds to Morecambe.

CHAPTER 14: THE SUPERHERO WITHIN

Reclining in a deck chair by a swimming pool whilst on a package holiday on a distant Greek island, The Pro flicks through his phone and sees the draw for the Carling Cup is due to be made later that day. He sets an alarm to watch the draw live before jumping into the pool to cool off. At 3pm the alarm buzzes and he tunes in to the two former professionals pour the balls from a velvet bag into a bowl and give them a stir. The third home team to be drawn is his hometown team, the same club that released him after 7 years of commitment without even a sideways glance. Come on thinks The Pro, come on. The ex-pro dips his hand into the bowl and pulls out a black marble ball, with the number 17 drawn on it.

"And they'll face League Two's Morecambe at home in August" narrates the presenter.

The Pro jumps up out of his chair, exclaming his delight to the somewhat confused fellow holiday makers relaxing by the pool, before divebombing into the water and further disrupting the serenity of the poolside atmosphere.

To The Pro, it is symbolic of his football career coming full circle. He sets this game as a huge target to aim for. His family, friends and doubters will be there, his mentor and no doubt the college tutor too. Wow. It's the way football and life play's out, thinks The Pro. Playing at the hometown stadium in a cup game, the same stadium he spent hours sat watching from the stands, where he dreamed of himself running out as a player throughout his entire childhood. And now, the God's of fate had drawn his team away in the first round of the Cup. The draw dreams are made of.

The first day of pre-season is tough. Then it gets tougher. And tougher. Being around senior professionals at the sharp end of the football league system is an eye opener. They have families to provide for, mortgages to pay, hardened experience and hundreds of league appearances combined with the desperate nature of 1-year contracts to keep their careers active. Professional football is competitive by its very nature, yet at this bottom end of the English football league system, the bruising reality is that its dog eat dog, even amongst teammates. Despite this, The Pro is still excited to be there, relishing each day training under a manager who retained legendary status amongst Manchester United fans and colleagues who had played in the Premier League.

The pre-season games start in earnest and The Pro is actively involved in all of them, starting half of the fixtures and featuring against Premier League teams in the higher profile games too. It's a far cry from the trial period at Fleetwood Town the year before, where he was a bit part at best two tiers below this level. As the first game of the League Two season got ever closer, The Pro was confident of being in the squad and possibly making his debut around the start of the season. Then the reality of professional football came home to roost. The week of the first league game, at the Monday morning training session, a trialist joined. The trialist was the former first team captain at his youth team club, a vastly experienced and very good centre back. The next day, the club announced the 1 year signing of said trialist, as well as a holding midfielder straight from the Scottish Premier League. Pushed down the pecking order, The Pro maintained his positive attitude and steady performances, despite his debut seemingly further away than two days prior.

The Pro is named on the bench for the first 4 league games and the lower league cup games. He doesn't get on the pitch as the team make a bright start to the campaign, punching well above their weight in the play-off places. Then the Carling Cup game falls next on the fixture list, away at his hometown club. The big one for Morecambe, but the huge one for The Pro personally. He is once again named on the bench. As he runs out for the pre match warm up in the cavernous stadium, he once again thinks how far he has come. Four years ago, this very club released him into the footballing abyss, one year ago he was 2 miles down the road frying McNuggets at the city centre McDonalds and now here he was, running out in an official cup game at the stadium he had called home since he was 4.

As The Pro's hometown team race to an early lead, and then cement it by going 5-0 up with 20 minutes to go, the manager looks around to the bench, instructing him and another young pro to get warmed up. There is only one substitution left to make and The Pro is certain he'll get the nod. He conducts an excited warm up on the touchline, hearing his schoolmates shout his name and spotting his family looking proud in the stands too. The manager shouts a name and The Pro and the other young pro bolt back to the dugout. The Pro takes off his jumper and steps forward, ready to fulfil his immediate dream. A debut, at his hometown team.

"Not you Rory son, sit back down." relays the assistant manager.

The Pro's heart stops. His soul slips. He had danced with his dream and had been left standing bereft. The other players on the bench snigger at him, banter being the justification for the heartless reactions.

"F*** off!" hissed The Pro as he slumped back into the seat in the away team dugout as the other young pro did a couple of knee tucks and sprinted onto the pitch to occupy his place on the hallowed turf. The Pro felt the adrenaline drain out of him, pit of latent anger erupting from the surface of years of rejection. He throws his shinpads in disgust, losing any sense of composure. The other players continue to take the proverbial out of him. As the final whistle blows, he trudges back to the changing room, head down, feet trailing, wanting the ground to swallow him up.

The next day he knocks on the manager's office door.

"Come in" invites the managers voice from behind the plywood door.

"Gaffer.." exhales The Pro, nerves mounting.

"You OK son?" asks the manager, oblivious to The Pro's evident upset.

"Do you know how much it would have meant to me to play just one-minute last night? It's my team I've supported them since I was 4, I'm from there, I..I….I" stutters The Pro, tears welling in his eyes.

"Calm down son. If you'd have told me maybe we could have got you on. I didn't know, I put the other kid on because we're 5-0 down and it wouldn't have been fair to put you on in defence in that situation. Hey, you're doing well, keep working hard and your chance will come" reassured the manager.

The next week, The Pro receives a copy of the computer game FIFA, with his own character detailed on the game. It goes on the bedroom shelf at home, next to the Football Manager games he features in, childhood trophies and framed shirts. Soon after he is loaned out to a local non-league team Kendal Town, three tiers below League Two. Many of the same players from Fleetwood play for Kendal, all less than impressed when they see their new loanee turn up for training before the FA Cup 2nd qualifying round that Saturday. The Pro is still running off anger though, and a certain sense of betrayal. The manager had promised him a chance, yet here he was a couple of weeks later, on loan and a million miles away from his debut. The FA Cup game is his first game for Kendal and he puts in a man of the match performance, full of aggression, competitiveness and desire. The match finishes in a 2-2 draw and a replay is scheduled for the following Tuesday. He's arrived in the blood and thunder of men's football that's for sure, with a broken nose to show for it, as he joins the rest of the team in drinking a beer or two on the back of the bus home. His performance teaches him a valuable lesson. The respect he craves must be earnt.

The loan spell is successful. Kendal find themselves on course to push for promotion around the top of the table and in the 4th round of the FA Cup qualifying round. The club request to extend the loan agreement for a further 2 months. The Pro speaks to Morecambe's manager.

"You can stay there son yes. Keep training with us, and keep up your community coaching duties too..." states the Gaffer.

The Pro has been assigned a role with the other younger pro's to deliver the football in the community programme for the club in local schools. Despite being a notoriously arduous fulfilment, The Pro enjoys engaging with his coaching practice again. Some of the older Pro's once again mock the younger players as they set off home for the afternoon and the younger lads load bags of dirty footballs into their small car boots. It's part and parcel of the pathway thinks The Pro as he wistfully smiles and heads to the local primary school before heading to Kendal training that evening.

At the end of the extended loan spell, he is recalled to Morecambe who have an injury crisis. He goes back to sitting on the bench in the freezing winter, the reserve fixtures getting called off week after week and his match fitness draining at an exponential rate. Then, a modern disaster strikes via an innocuous interaction on social media. A Facebook friend request comes through from a female with two mutual friends, two of his England schoolboy teammates. He accepts. Up pops a message.

-Hi, do you play for Morecambe? - asks the stranger.

-Hey, yes, I do, how come? - types back The Pro.

-Oh, I'm the managers step daughter- with a smiley face emoji comes the response.

At this point The Pro knows he's in grave danger, messaging his old teammates to verify the information just provided, knowing full well this interaction, if true, can only spell disaster.

-Yeah mate, she said she's his step daughter and when I said you played for Morecambe, she said she'd add you, why what's up? - replies one of the England teammates.

-Ah ok, no worries just thought it's a bit weird- responds The Pro.

-Hey, my step Dad's just got home, I'll go and ask him how you're doing- pops up a message from the dangerous stranger.

-You don't have to do that- desperately responds The Pro.

Two minutes later another message pops up.

-I just asked him, he said he knows you and he'll see you at training tomorrow smiley face emoji-

The Pro knows this is bad news. He knows the toxic masculinity and macho culture of professional football won't allow the manager to let this innocent interaction slide and a tirade of abuse is coming in the office the following morning.

On the way to training he tells his trusted allies, the incredibly supportive Goalkeeper and club captain who is his mentor in chief at the club, as well as the other two regular car school teammates. By the time the players head out from the changing room to train, the story has spread like wildfire and Chinese whispers have transformed a Facebook interaction into a full-blown explicit relationship. The Pro squirms as the manager lines up the players to address them, an out of the ordinary occurrence. He walks down the line of players before stopping in front of The Pro.

"You!" he bellows, thrusting his finger in The Pro's face.

"That's too f***ing close to home! Don't you ever speak to her again!" he continues to shout, spit landing on The Pro's face.

"I didn't…" starts The Pro.

"Don't say another word! My office after training…" the manager cuts in before storming back to the changing area to shouts from the rest of the lads.

"He's been smashing her for weeks gaffer..."
"Told us he's coming yours for tea tomorrow night gaffer..."
"Anything to get in the team gaffer..."

“Said she’s great up top gaffer...”

Come the uncouth comments from the lads as the manager gets out of earshot.

“You’re screwed mate” whispers the goalkeeper ally, putting an arm round his shoulder in a kinship.

By the end of the training session the manager has already left the training ground. He spends more time in the Sky Sports News studio than the training ground so it’s no real surprise. The next day The Pro is called into the manager’s office. The manager isn’t there but his assistant is.

“You’ve really upset him son…” explains the assistant, “ He’s going to punish you so just take the medicine and focus on the football, it’ll take him a while to calm down” he continues.

“I literally did nothing wrong. She’s added me, messaged me and there’s nothing wrong in it?” proclaims The Pro.

The next day he is sent out on loan until the end of the season to a team two tiers below League Two, to a club battling relegation. It’s a tough environment, a weak team in a strong league. He plays well, helps them pick up some good results and avoid relegation, at the same time as Morecambe go on an unbelievable run to their highest ever league position and qualify for the League Two play offs. His loan spell ends and he returns to Morecambe. The first leg of the play off semi-final ends in a huge 5-1 defeat, rendering the second leg almost redundant as a spectacle. Morecambe win the second leg 1-0 at home but miss out on a final at Wembley.

By 5pm the following day, Sky Sports News announce the released lists from each League Two club, the names running across the bottom of the tv screen in a yellow banner for over an hour. No one from the club has contacted him. No one said anything to the younger pro's after the game. No one spoke about any more training or end of season do's. It just ended. But there, in a solid black text against the familiar yellow background rolling across the screen sits the name Rory Winters in the released list. It's all so familiar.

Lesson 14: The Superhero Within

Every football career will come to an end one day. You can be the best player in the world, a third-choice goalkeeper, a perennial winner or a mediocre mid table substitute; one day it'll all end. You'll no longer be needed. And it generally happens in the blink of an eye, as it did for me. One day, a professional footballer, wrapped up in the egotistical world of a full-time athlete, the next literally unemployed, lost and incredibly upset. It's cruel and it's inevitable.

Being prepared for what's next is essential. This isn't the end of you, your story, your life. It's the end of one fantastic chapter, one which will inform the rest of the beautiful story you are creating. Using football as a tool for positive outcomes is the ideal way to reframe 'the end' into the start of something new.

I outlined in the previous chapters how I went from Rory, who enjoyed football as a young boy, to The Pro, a high school superhero who was lauded by his classmates as positively different. As with any superhero story, there has to be a villain too. The bad guy in my story was often a coach, a teammate I was competing with or an opponent I faced. These battles left me far removed from the only villain I had to defeat all along. Myself. I really had no special powers other than raw talent coupled with the dedication and discipline to become a professional footballer, but it's hard as a teenager to navigate that journey without the correct guidance and advice in place.

This book is a snapshot of my own story, the development of which has involved using football to my advantage and not letting football use me. After I left the professional game, the competencies, skills and resilience, superpowers some might say, that I had built up from a childhood and young adulthood spent in professional football served me incredibly well. I was driven, focused and uncompromising in my pursuit of excellence. I was also still hardwired to compete, but out there in the 'real world' success was defined by more than winning. The lack of 'villains' outside of professional football meant oftentimes I pitted myself against myself. This had both positive and negative effects on my personal development.

I came to acknowledged that The Pro has never been a superhero. In fact, when I was released from Morecambe without so much as a goodbye at the age of 20, I was just a very lost young man who struggled to find genuine happiness for years. I have since spent a lot of time, energy and money investing in my mental health through therapy, courses and education. My identity was bruised and battered and as a result I threw myself into academia, gaining top marks in my degree, Master's degree and securing amazing teaching jobs in England and across the globe. I was trying to prove myself to the world, to my family and friends, but most of all to myself. It was an endless chase of being good enough for someone, anyone. It was tiring.

The switch flicked not too long ago for me. I lost a former teammate to suicide and realised that I too has battled my own demons related to being a purported 'failure' as a footballer. Another close friend then suffered a collapse in his own mental health which he directly correlates to being at a Premier League academy until 16 and not 'making it' thereafter. It's my journey, and it's 98% of other academy footballers stories too. It's a brutal path that leaves far too many young people bereft and alone. My whole goal now is to change this narrative for all young footballers who have so much to offer the world either on or beyond a grass field.

I found a mentor myself, someone who had been through the same journey as me and come out stronger for it, and I immediately felt a weight lift from my shoulders. Learning that it's OK to just be me allowed me to feel more liberated than any job, degree classification or external achievement ever could. It is this liberation that I'd like to pass on to others, to help them emerge far stronger than they think is possible.

AFTERWORD

Rory Winters, The Pro, would not be defined by his rejections in football.

By a stroke of luck, the physio at Morecambe pulled a few strings which enabled him to enrol on a Sport & Exercise Science degree at Edge Hill University in Liverpool, England.

His desire to pursue education and football remained strong. So did his sense of adventure. By 2012 he was 2 years into a degree, a regular for Kendal Town FC for 2 seasons before following his adventurous spirit and thriving playing soccer in America for National Premier Soccer League team AFC Cleveland. He was recognised in the national team of the year and shortlisted for national player of the year. He loved playing football abroad, inspired by the Argentinians in Bangladesh. Graduating with first class honours degree from Edge Hill was followed by another life changing spell playing abroad, this time in Canada with FC London, the reigning United Soccer League National champions. It was an experience that would give him lifelong friends all over the world, from Colombia to Australia, Mexico to Germany.

Returning to the UK, Rory embarked upon a full scholarship Master's degree in Coaching Science at the outstanding sports university, Hartpury. He combined studying with playing for Gloucester City in the National League North and a role as Athletic Development Manager for 6 of thr professional football club academies based in the South West of England. During this time, he also completed his UEFA B Coaching Licence. Combining a high level of study, playing and coaching stimulated his thirst for challenge and continued development.

He then completed a Physical Education teaching qualification in his hometown and played for Lancaster City FC and Kendal Town FC again. Upon qualifying as a teacher, he was appointed as Director of Strength and Conditioning and Football lead coach at Northampton School for Boys, the top ranked state school for sport in England. Here, he mentored, coached and taught an array of elite level athletes in Athletics, Dance, Rugby and Football, most notably Carney Chukwuemeka, a £20 million signing for Chelsea in the summer of 2022. He also continued to play football at a high level with AFC Rushden & Diamonds.

Seeing an opportunity to move abroad to further his football and coaching acumen, as well as satisfy his itch to see the world, he moved to Singapore in 2017. Two years as an elite level S&C Coach at Asia's best gym led to a spell working for the English Premier League as a fitness auditor for 4 months before returning to Singapore to launch Edge of the Box Mentoring. To date, Rory has worked with over 60 professional football players in Singapore, with 17 professional debuts made, 12 international debuts and countless other lives changed amongst both female and male footballers. Through EOTB, Rory also held positions as Director of Football at Singapore FC, Tanglin Trust International School and as Assistant Coach at Singapore Premier League club Balestier Khalsa FC.

'The Pro' also came full circle whilst in Singapore and made one last appearance- for a Premier League club! He returned to the elite level of football for one game at the Singapore National Stadium, playing for Liverpool alongside Luis Garcia and Emile Heskey against Manchester United FC, marking Dmitar Berbatov. So, by following his dream and remaining true to himself, however unconventional it may have been, The Pro did eventually play for a Premier League team, 16 years after being told he'd never be good enough to.

In early 2023, Rory returned to London to bring EOTB to footballers in the UK, with the ambition to show them how they can utilise football to change their world.

To find out more about this incredible journey and how Rory developed his mantra that every player should:

"Use Football To Your Advantage, Don't Let Football Use You"

You can reach Rory via email at:
eotbmentoring@gmail.com

or on social media at @eotbmentoring

Rory Winters
The Pro

Printed in Great Britain
by Amazon

23615895R00066